This idealistic portrait of Giacomo Costantino Beltrami served as the frontispiece for the 1828 London edition of his book.

GIACOMO COSTANTINO BELTRAMI
(About 1814)

THE MAN WITH THE RED UMBRELLA

THE MAN WITH THE RED UMBRELLA:

Giacomo Costantino Beltrami in America

BY

AUGUSTO P. MICELI

CLAITOR'S PUBLISHING DIVISION
BATON ROUGE, LOUISIANA

Library of Congress Catalog
Card Number: 73–93581

Printed in the United States of America
by The TJM Corporation
Baton Rouge, Louisiana

To
Virginia

PREFACE

I "MET" GIACOMO COSTANTINO BELtrami by accident. While studying a map of Minnesota, I noted Beltrami County. How did this Italian name find its way to Minnesota? A search in several encyclopedias yielded a scanty biography of Beltrami. It stated that he had traveled alone in the wilds of Minnesota and ultimately reached New Orleans where, in 1824, he published a book in French about his travels. To my delight, I discovered that Tulane University in New Orleans had a copy of this rare volume, *La Découverte des Sources du Mississippi, etc.* It was a fascinating find. This launched me on the project of retracing the life of this extraordinary Italian and I have continued since that day in 1964. My purpose was to rescue Beltrami's memory from comparative obscurity. Whenever my professional duties allowed me, I followed Beltrami in his travels and adventures, both in his books and by visiting the places where he had been. In 1969, I went to Bemidji, the County Seat of Beltrami County in Minnesota. As far as the roads permitted, I followed Beltrami's trail, from Red River Lake to Lake Julia, Turtle

Lake and down the Mississippi River to St. Paul and Minneapolis.

Subsequently, I visited the Italian's native city of Bergamo in Northern Italy, where I found Beltrami's manuscripts, documents, Indian artifacts and the red umbrella which he carried in and out of the Wilderness. I returned to this picturesque city three other times, and later visited Macerata where Beltrami sat as a judge and Filottrano where he died.

In the years I devoted to Beltrami, many persons have generously assisted me.

I am under great obligation to the staff of Tulane University's Howard-Tilton Library, especially Mrs. Connie Griffith of the Manuscript Division and Mrs. Dorothy Whittemore of the Reference Department. Without their authoritative guidance and cooperative assistance, this book could not have been written. Much assistance was also cheerfully given by the staffs of the New Orleans Public Library, the Louisiana State Museum Library and the library of Loyola University.

Many courtesies were extended to me by the Minnesota Historical Society in St. Paul, and I am particularly grateful to Mrs. June D. Holmquist, managing editor of *Minnesota History* for her interest, significant suggestions and encouragement. In Bemidji, Minn. Mr. C. L. Johnson, an officer of the Beltrami County Historical Society, was also most helpful, as was Mrs. Alice Bonners.

In Philadelphia, the staffs of the Historical Society of Pennsylvania and the American Philosophical Society made available to me pertinent materials in their vast collections, while similar courteous services were accorded me by the New-York Historical Society and the New York Public Library.

Considerable research was conducted in Italy, where Beltrami manuscripts, memorabilia, artifacts and earlier studies of his career were found in Bergamo, his native city, and at Macerata and Filottrano. At Bergamo, extensive assistance was provided by Prof. Antonio Valle, director of the Museo di Scienze Naturali; Signorina Dora Coggiola of the Biblioteca Civica A.Maj; Fausto Asperti, eminent photographer; and Sandro Angelini, distinguished architect.

Count Glauco Luchetti, who lives in Beltrami's villa at Filottrano, made available to me his vast collection of Beltrami papers, books and personal articles, and for his gracious and invaluable assistance I am in his debt.

A particular kindness was shown me by Dr. Nicola Marchesini of Macerata in supplying background materials on the period when Beltrami resided in that city. I wish also to thank the Dante Alighieri Society in Rome for providing me with a copy of Beltrami's will.

Beauregard Bassich put his expert knowledge of photography at my disposal, and has my gratitude for his generous assistance.

Finally, I wish to express my deep thanks to my friend, Charles L. Dufour, *States-Item* columnist and author, who supplied enthusiastic prodding when the project lagged and whose suggestions were readily accepted in preparing the final manuscript. I am also grateful for the time he spent in reading proof and checking references.

In acknowledging the invaluable assistance I have received from so many persons, I assume full responsibility for any errors that may have escaped detection.

To my "Beltrami-widow," Virginia, I express my gratitude for the hours, days, weeks, months and years when she so patiently permitted Giacomo Costantino Beltrami to be a part of our household.

New Orleans, La. AUGUSTO P. MICELI
January 28, 1974

CONTENTS

THE MAN WITH THE RED UMBRELLA

CHAPTER ONE

"Men Will Dispose of My Name . . ."

DUSK ENVELOPED THE CENTURY-OLD city as the *Dolphin* eased to the levee at New Orleans. While the steamboat from St. Louis tied up in the forest of smokestacks and masts on that December day in 1823, one of the passengers, standing among the baggage and the bales of peltries on the crowded deck, contemplated the scene about him. Giacomo Costantino Beltrami, jurist, soldier, classical scholar, traveler, writer, patriot, political dreamer, and exile from his native Italy, had just completed a journey down the Mississippi River from its source almost to the mighty stream's mouth. By foot through the wilderness, by canoe on hazardous rivers, and finally by steamboat, Beltrami had traveled more than 3,000 miles in six adventure-crowded months among Indians, both friendly and hostile, fur-traders and trappers, garrisons of isolated army posts, and the vast silences of the northern forests.

Beltrami, who had served the Emperor Napoleon in both a military and judicial capacity, was imbued with liberal ideas which had rendered him suspect after the fall of the Corsican and the Congress of Vienna. He shared

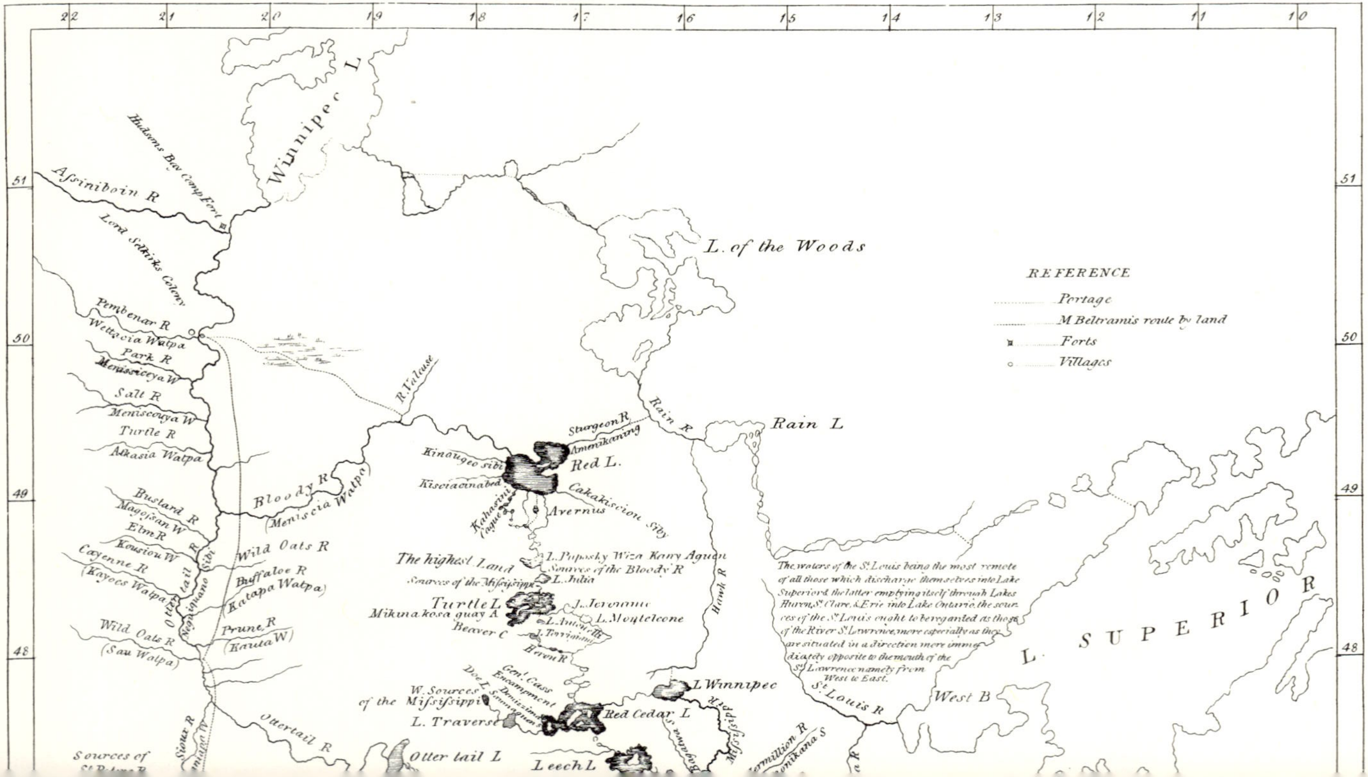

REFERENCE
Portage
M Beltrami's route by land
Forts
Villages
L. of the Woods
Winnipec L
Hudsons Bay Comp Fort
Assiniboin R
Lord Selkirks Colony
Pembenar R
Wettacia Watpa
Park R
Menissiceya W
Salt R
Meniscouya W
Turtle R
Alkasia Watpa
R.Valeuse
Bloody R
Meniscia Watpa
Bustard R
Magojsan W
Elm R
Kousiou W
Cayenne R
(Kayecs Watpa)
Wild Oats R
Buffaloe R
Katapa Watpa)
Prune R
(Kauta W)
Wild Oats R
(Sau Watpa)
Negniguano Sibi
Ottertail R
Sioux R
Sources of
Rain R
Rain L
Sturgeon R
Amenikaning
Red L.
Kinaugeo sibi
Kisciacinabed
Cakakiscion Siby
Avernus
The highest Land
L. Puposky Wiza Kany Aguen
Sources of the Bloody R
Sources of the Missisippi
L. Julia
Turtle L
Mikunakosa quay A
L. Jeronimo
L. Monteleone
Beaver C
Heron R
Hawk R
Gen! Cass Encampment
Doe L
W. Sources of the Missisippi
L. Traverse
Red Cedar L
L. Winnipec
Missisippi R
Otter tail L
Leech L
The waters of the St. Louis being the most remote of all those which discharge themselves into Lake Superior & the latter emptying itself through Lakes Huron, St. Clare, & Erie into Lake Ontario, the sources of the St. Louis ought to be regarded as those of the River St. Lawrence, more especially as they are situated in a direction more immediately opposite to the mouth of the St. Lawrence namely from West to East.
St. Louis R
West B
L. SUPERIOR
Vermillion R

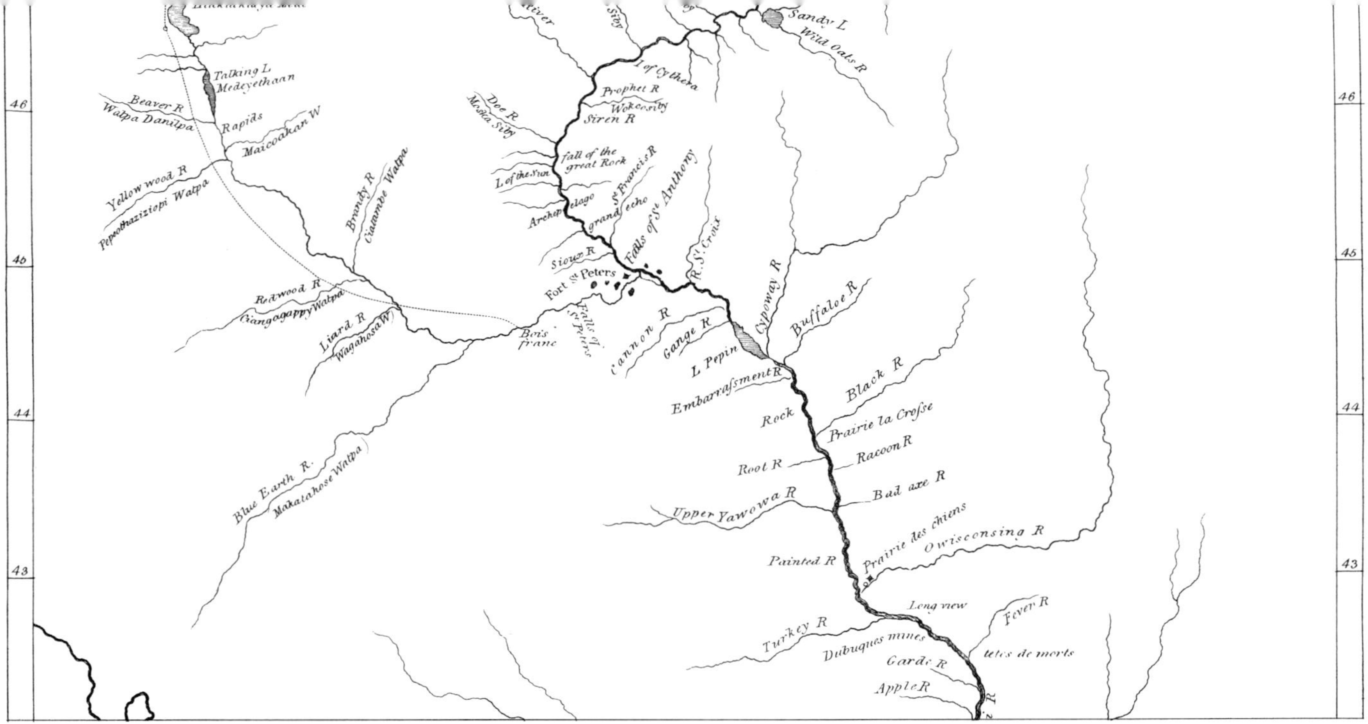

Map of Beltrami's travels, from 1828 London Edition of "A Pilgrimage in Europe and America, etc.," Vol II.

with many the dream of a united Italy and it was inevitable, after several incidents with the authorities and arrests on suspicion of political subversion, that exile, either imposed or voluntary, should be his lot.

He had begun his travels in October, 1821. After traveling in France, Germany, Belgium, and England, he embarked at Liverpool on October 25, 1822, for Philadelphia, because he did not want to "stagnate in London or Paris" when he could travel to America, where "the virtues which enabled [the Americans] to triumph over European oppression are yet in all their freshness." [1]

Beltrami landed in Philadelphia on December 30, 1822. There he lost no time in engaging a printer to publish a book of his European travels, *Deux Mots sur des Promenades de Paris à Liverpool.*[2] He visited Baltimore and Washington (where he called on President James Monroe), and journeyed by stagecoach to Pittsburgh. From there he planned to travel down the Ohio and Mississippi to New Orleans.

A fortuitous meeting at the confluence of the Ohio and the Mississippi with Major Lawrence Taliaferro, Indian agent at Fort St. Anthony (later Fort Snelling in Minneapolis and St. Paul), caused Beltrami to alter his plans and determined him to join the major's party for the purpose of visiting the Indian tribes and studying their customs. Later, the idea seized him to plunge into the wilderness in search of the source of the Mississippi. Beltrami carried in his baggage a large red umbrella, which not only sheltered his supplies during rainstorms but also proved a picturesque passport to safety among hostile Indians. Thus equipped, Beltrami struck off into the North American wilds. Ultimately he located what he believed to be the northernmost source of the Mississippi and named it Lake Julia in memory of a close friend, Countess Giulia Spada de Medici.

When he had completed these explorations in what is now the state of Minnesota, Beltrami decided to resume his deferred voyage to New Orleans. After reaching St. Louis, he embarked on the *Dolphin* on November 9, 1823. As the boat steamed toward New Orleans—a trip that took longer than a month—he organized his notes and prepared a manuscript for publication. In March, 1824, Benjamin Levy, a New Orleans printer, published in French Beltrami's book, *La Découverte des Sources du Mississippi et de la Rivière Sanglante.*[3]

Although Beltrami was the friend or correspondent of some of the leading political and literary figures of the day—letters from Lafayette, Thomas Jefferson, Chateaubriand, and Benjamin Constant are in the Beltrami papers in the municipal library in his native Bergamo—and although his book was printed in an English edition in London in 1828 and was praised by the New Orleans, New York, London, and Paris press, both the man and his book are little remembered today. However, the state of Minnesota has perpetuated the memory of Giacomo Costantino Beltrami. In 1866, one of the largest counties was named for him, and within this county is Lake Beltrami. A village of Beltrami still exists in Polk County, and geological maps show Beltrami Island in a glacial lake. In the City of Minneapolis, there is a park that also bears his name.

Whenever modern writers revive Beltrami's memory, however briefly, the tendency has been to treat him only as a quixotic character. Yet this image, while in part true, is far from the full picture of the man. Beltrami was, indeed, by American frontier standards "different," and he could prove difficult because of an excess of pride, a tendency to boastfulness, a short temper, and an impatience with compromising truth and honesty. But Beltrami had a keen mind, unflagging energy, and an insatiable curiosity, which transcended any quixotic characteristics.

Before returning to Europe in 1826, Beltrami visited Mexico and Haiti. The former journey resulted in a two-volume work on Mexico, published in Paris in 1830.[4] He resided in London, Paris, and in the Neckar Valley in Germany, and returned to Italy in 1837. Although in bad health, he lived nearly two decades longer on his estate at Filottrano, where he died on January 6, 1855.

As the years passed and new events and new discoveries took the stage, Beltrami's contributions to travel, exploration, and the world of letters were virtually forgotten. "After my death," he wrote, with a resignation which was uncharacteristic, ". . . men will dispose of my name, as God will of my soul, according as I shall have well or ill deserved during my life; and I leave to my friends and to those who have had opportunities of becoming acquainted with my heart, the charge of defending my memory, should it ever be attacked by injustice or prejudice."[5]

CHAPTER TWO

The Man from Bergamo

THE SIXTEENTH OF THE SEVENTEEN children of Giovanni Battista Beltrami and Margherita Carozzi was born in 1779 in Bergamo, an old town situated in the foothills of the Italian Alps. From Bergamo sprang such diverse figures as Bartolomeo Colleoni, fifteenth-century condottiere and captain-general of the Republic of Venice; Gaetano Donizetti, nineteenth-century operatic composer; and Angelo Giuseppe Roncalli, better known as John XXIII, beloved twentieth-century pope.

The boy was baptized Giacomo Costantino Beltrami in the church of Santa Eufemia. The records of this church were destroyed by fire in 1793, so the exact dates of his birth and baptism cannot be determined. Although little is known of Beltrami's youth, his father, as chief customs officer of the Venetian republic, had the means to provide his children with a good education. Young Giacomo seems to have been well grounded in Greek and Latin literature, among other subjects. The elder Beltrami had planned a career in the law for Giacomo, but the invasion of the French under Napoleon into northern Italy in 1796 intervened. Beltrami, only eighteen, enlisted in the militia of the new Cisalpine Republic. His promotions were rapid and within a few years he became vice-inspector of the armies.

In 1807, Beltrami was appointed chancellor of the Department of Justice of Parma, and he later occupied a similar post at Udine, after which he was appointed judge at Macerata.[1] In 1813, because of ill health, he took a leave of absence and spent several months in Florence. In the Tuscan city Beltrami was introduced into the salon of the Countess Louise d'Albany, widow of Prince Charles Edward Stuart, the "Young Pretender."

In her palace on the Arno, the Countess d'Albany presided over one of Europe's most famous salons. Here came noted artists, distinguished men of letters, and important political personages. Beltrami found himself in intimate contact with such men as Alphonse Lamartine, François Chateaubriand, Antonio Canova, Lord John Russell, Lord Byron, Ugo Foscolo, and Diego Pignatelli, Duke of Monteleone. Pignatelli, a descendant of Hernando Cortez, discussed his Mexican property with Beltrami and suggested that perhaps he might undertake a legal mission to Mexico for him. It was perhaps Pignatelli who first stimulated Beltrami's interest in America.

The circle in which Beltrami moved was well depicted by Lamartine's description of the Countess d'Albany's salon: "After dinner we entered the salon, where around the Countess each evening illustrious men . . . met. I listened with rapt curiosity to the names as they were announced by the [liveried] servant[s], names of families which history had taught me to know and names of professors and men of letters, then new to me. As they arrived they sat in a semicircle around a small table loaded with piles of books behind which was the countess semireclining on a sofa." During the academic discussion which ensued the nineteen-year-old Lamartine remained "silent and cold as the chair on which he sat." [2]

When Beltrami finally returned to Macerata he found that several judges, in whom he reposed no confidence, had been appointed to his court. He promptly resigned. The Imperial Commission was reluctant to accept his resignation, but Beltrami stubbornly refused to withdraw it. He retired to his estate at nearby Filottrano.[3]

Events in 1815 profoundly affected Beltrami's future. With the fall of Napoleon and the crumbling of the French empire, Bergamo became a part of the Lombardo Veneto kingdom under Austrian domination, and Filottrano and Macerata were annexed to the Papal States. This parcelling of Italy was a severe setback to the hopes of those, including Beltrami, who dreamed of a united Italy. Moreover, it placed him in an ambiguous position when he was called upon to take an oath of allegiance to the provisional government, pending the annexation by the Papal States.

In open court on July 2, 1815, Beltrami refused to take the oath of allegiance. As one who had "alienated all property elsewhere, except in this region," he declared that he subscribed to the doctrine *ubi bona, ibi patria* ("where the property, there the fatherland"), and believed that he "should therefore be considered a citizen and subject after seven years of honorable residence." Noting that published reports indicated the region would soon be returned to the authority of the Supreme Pontiff, Beltrami protested his fealty "to whomsoever God gives me as a sovereign," but would not so swear. "Firm and unalterable, at all times and in all circumstances, regarding the principles of Morality, Religion and Honor . . . yet I cannot in honesty swear the oath demanded of me." [4]

Clearly, Beltrami sought the protection of his person and property without taking an oath that would com-

Countess d'Albany—born Louise Maximiliana Caroline de Stolberg—was the widow of Charles Edward Stuart, the "Young Pretender" to the English Throne. Her salon, to which the young Beltrami had access, was one of the most famous of Europe.

promise his dedication to a united Italy. When activities of the Carbonari—the secret revolutionary organization dedicated to a united Italy—came under official scrutiny at Macerata, many suspected persons were arrested. A revolt had been planned for the night of the feast of St. John (June 24–25, 1817), in concert with similar groups in Ancona and Bologna. Beltrami, in the light of his refusal to take the oath, fell under suspicion and was ordered out of the region. Despite the fact that he was temporarily crippled and forced to use crutches, as the result of a fall from a horse, Beltrami was compelled to leave immediately. He sought a haven in Florence, where the Countess d'Albany and other old friends received him warmly.[5]

While Beltrami was in exile in Florence, criminal charges were filed against him at Rome. It was alleged that he practiced no religion and was a Mason—serious charges by a reactionary regime—and that he had profiteered in wheat. Rather than risk conviction in absentia, and confiscation of his properties, Beltrami decided to go to Rome to face the charges. Powerful friends came to his defense. The Countess d'Albany enlisted the aid of Count d'Appony, Austrian minister in Florence. Claiming that Beltrami, who had been born in Bergamo, was now, with the restoration, a citizen of the Austria-Hungarian empire, the countess insisted that the accusations against Beltrami were unfounded, although she conceded he had been unwise when, during Napoleon's ascendancy, he had purchased church property which had been seized and put up for sale.[6] Beltrami was acquitted and permitted to return unchallenged to Filottrano in May, 1818.

During his residence at Macerata, Beltrami formed a platonic friendship with the Countess Giulia Spada de Medici. Giulia de Medici was a woman of great charm, culture, and intellectual accomplishments. Herself a poet, she was a member of the Accademia dei Catenati, a liter-

PASSAPORTO
ALL' ESTERO.

Registro 4: 1813.
N.° 406 . . . . . .

CONNOTATI.

Età d'a 35 Anni
Statura alta
Capegli grelli
Fronte giusta
Sopracciglia oscure
Occhi castagni
Naso grosso
Bocca regolare
Barba oscura
Mento tondo
Viso lungo
Colorito vivace

MARCHE PARTICOLARI.

SOTTOSCRIZIONE DEL LATORE

Prefetto DEL MUSONE 40

AVVERTENZE NECESSARIE.

Tanto nel sortire dal Regno, quanto nel rientrarvi il latore del presente è tenuto di farlo vidimare dall' Ispettore di Polizia, o Viceprefetto o Prefetto che risiede più vicino alla frontiera lungo lo stradale rispettivo.

All' estero deve presentarsi per lo stesso effetto, agli Ambasciatori Ministri, Incaricati d' affari, od altri Agenti diplomatici o consolari del Regno, ed in loro mancanza, agli Agenti sotto i detti titoli di S. M. l' Imperatore dei Francesi, che risiedessero nel luogo di suo soggiorno.

Polizia Generale del Regno.

IN NOME

di S. M. Napoleone I,

Imperatore de' Francesi e Re d' Italia

Noi Michele Villata Prefetto del Dipartimento del Musone

Partendo da Macerata Il Sig.r Giacomo Costantino Beltrami

di condizione . . . nativo di Bergamo
Dipartimento del Serio domiciliato in Macerata
Dipartimento del Musone per recarsi a Foligno
in compagnia di Domenico Ciarampino d'anni 35 suo domestico

Invitiamo tutti gli Officiali Civili e Militari del Regno, e preghiamo quelli delle Potenze amiche a lasciarli liberamente passare, e prestargli ajuto e protezione in caso di bisogno.

Il presente Passaporto accordato per Anno uno vale per giorni trenta per sortire dal Territorio del Regno d' Italia, e si rilascia sopra piena Conoscenza Personale.

Dato in Macerata il 1. Ottobre 1813.
Per il Prefetto ass.
Il Segretario Generale

Il Segretario Generale

Tassa lire due oltre il bollo.

Passport issued to Beltrami by the Napoleonic Kingdom of Italy in 1813.

ary society founded in 1574, which once included among its members Torquato Tasso. The countess was given the nom de plume of *Dama della Croce Stellata* ("Lady of the Starred Cross"). When she died in 1820, Beltrami experienced a melancholy which, he wrote, never fully left him thereafter. An elegy he composed in her memory gained him admission into the Accademia dei Catenati. His nom de plume was Alcandro Grineo.[7]

The years 1820 and 1821 were heavy with sadness for Beltrami. Revolts organized by the Carbonari broke out in Naples and Turin. After an initial success, these were crushed by the intervention of Austrian troops. Through these difficult times, advocates of Italian independence continued to plan the liberation and unification of Italy. Leading men of letters lent their pens to the cause. Ugo Foscolo refused to take the oath of allegiance, as Beltrami had, and fled to exile in England. Also seeking refuge in England were Giovanni Berchet and Gabriele Rossetti, father of the Pre-Raphaelite Dante Gabriel Rossetti. Alessandro Manzoni in Milan and the melancholy poet, Giacomo Leopardi, in Recanati (a few miles from Macerata), wrote patriotic poems, essays, and novels. Count Federico Gonfaloniere and Silvio Pellico were arrested and confined to prison in Austria.[8]

Beltrami's lingering grief over the death of the Countess de Medici; his frustrated hopes for a united Italy; and the constant surveillance by the Papal State's police to which he was subjected, made his stay in Filottrano unbearable. The idea of visiting distant lands had long been in his mind and his resentment of the existing political climate determined him to go abroad.[9]

Although the chief object of Beltrami's travels was to seek, as he wrote, "relief from the afflictions which oppress my heart," he already had the literary intention "by my feeble efforts, of presenting to my country . . . a consoling recollection of those high attempts and glorious achievements by which her children have very often astonished every country and every age."[10]

Leopardi's poem, "To Italy," published in that period, expressed well Beltrami's sadness and his desire to recapture for his country its past glories:

> O my country, I see the walls, the arches,
> the columns, the statues, the defenseless towers
> of our forefathers,
> But the glory, I do not see.[11]

Beltrami left Filottrano on October 1, 1821, and traveled to Assisi, Perugia, Siena, and Florence. In Florence he found the Countess d'Albany "still inconsolable" for the death of their dear friend, Giulia Spada de Medici, "the most perfect model of wife, mother, friend, and of every Christian virtue." After visiting Lucca, Pisa, Leghorn, and Chiavari, he reached Genoa, the city known for the "wondrous situation . . . the grandeur of its buildings; the beauty of its climate; and the loveliness of its women, with their delicate little hands and feet."[12]

Armed with letters of introduction from the Countess d'Albany to important people in Europe, Beltrami received police clearance in mid-December, 1821, to leave the country, and he departed for Paris.[13]

CHAPTER THREE

Tales of a Traveler

AS HIS HORSE PLODDED ALONG THE coast toward Ventimiglia, Beltrami regarded the foothills of the Maritime Alps, from whose summit in April, 1796, the young Bonaparte had pointed out to his weary soldiers the open road to Italy. A devoted follower of the victorious general, Beltrami was also an admirer of Napoleon in defeat. Napoleon's ultimate failure, Beltrami believed, was due to "the immensity and the universality of his projects that wrecked the whole. Had he been content to achieve and acquire less, he might have settled the policy of Europe." Not yet having heard of the death of Napoleon, he was eager to reach Toulon, "the cradle of the glory of the Prisoner of St. Helena."

Napoleon was very much in his mind as he left Nice after a short stay. "I cannot help feeling the liveliest interest in so great a man," he wrote, "an interest which no change of fortune can destroy." Beltrami did not linger long in Cannes, where, he recalled, "the reign of the hundred days began," but pushed on to Toulon. The twenty-four-year-old Bonaparte, a lieutenant colonel of artillery, had planned the attack on Toulon in 1793 and, Beltrami remarked, "in a great measure, directed the execution of it, by the superior management of his batteries, which mowed down the enemy in all directions." From Toulon five years later "the same little lieutenant-colonel of artillery . . . embarked in 1798 as general-in-chief, and as a victorious hero," bound for new exploits in Egypt.

An avid theatergoer, Beltrami attended Rossini's opera *The Barber of Seville* in Marseilles. The modern section of the city impressed him as "a delightful, rich, and commercial town." Yet he found "nothing in Marseilles which can fix the attention of a lover of the arts," and soon he was en route to Aix-en-Provence, over a bad road through a fine countryside. Aix, with its handsome avenues, walks, and houses, "is calculated to amuse a stranger for two or three days," Beltrami said.

At Arles, Beltrami had an encounter with the authorities which afforded him considerable amusement. One evening at the theater (which he found "modern and bad" with "actors . . . altogether *antique*"), he noticed "a great many inquisitive looks" directed at him. He observed that gendarmes had taken up positions within the theater. "I suspected immediately that the description of my person had deceived them in some way," he wrote, "and I bethought myself of encouraging them in their mistake, by way of a little diversion." Beltrami then "played the part of an embarrassed man," and noted the satisfied "countenances and gestures" which indicated to him that the police considered "that the bird was in the net."

When he had become "the principal sight in the theatre," he decided to terminate the game. He arose resolutely and passed through the inner door of the theater. But the door to the street was closed and blocked by gendarmes.

"What is the meaning of this?" demanded Beltrami.

"May I see Monsieur's passport?" asked the police commissioner.

"Only swindlers carry passports about them," replied Beltrami. "If you choose to see mine, you must come with me to my hotel."

The commissioner and six gendarmes escorted Beltrami to the hotel. "I showed him papers, as many as he pleased," wrote Beltrami, "and in the meantime I told him my mind about this disgraceful manner of annoying strangers." The crestfallen commissioner of police apologized profusely and showed Beltrami a circular with the description of a certain conspiratorial colonel of Besançon, a description which, Beltrami admitted, "corresponded in some particulars with mine."

Continuing through Provence, Beltrami visited Avignon, where its associations with Petrarch caused him to think about "the illustrious Italian who rescued literature and science from the darkness of past ages." Beltrami, who was deeply interested in Roman antiquities, was impressed by the amphitheater at Nimes. He considered it superior to the Coliseum in Rome and to the Arena in Verona "if we consider the gigantic stones of which it is composed, and the art with which they are joined without cement." The Pont du Gard was a "great exhibition of human industry . . . one of the most magnificent monuments of Roman greatness." Beltrami summed up in a sentence the impact of the massive aqueduct: "As soon as it breaks upon our sight, we stop and wonder; when we draw nearer, we wonder and stop."

Fifteen days after he had left Genoa, Beltrami found himself at Toulouse, a "gloomy" city which was, however, "the key of the Pyrenees." He continued his journey to Langon, on the Garonne, where he boarded a steamboat for the twenty-six-mile voyage to Bordeaux. His fellow travelers made an amusing party—"gay fellows who were at once Parisian and Gascon; . . . speculators, . . . politicians, . . . a sick lady, . . . a lady quite well, . . . Englishmen examining the moon in bright sunshine, and making almanacks; on one side singing and whistling, on another yawning and snoring; priests praying, sailors swearing; a German who spoke French, and a Frenchman who spoke German, I myself endeavouring to speak both languages, and the trio making the most harmonious jargon in the world. . . . In France, whether by land or by water, you always travel merrily, and sometimes agreeably . . . in general with amusing and well-behaved company."

From Bordeaux, Beltrami made a pilgrimage to the nearby Chateau of Brede, birthplace of Montesquieu, "that great luminary who has thrown light on the legislation of the whole world." He remained to see the carnival, three days of "bustle and joviality," with "masked processions of all ranks and classes, . . . people on horseback, in carriages, and on foot." On leaving Bordeaux, he traveled through Rochefort and La Rochelle to La Vendée, "the poorest and weakest province of France" in point of civilization, but the "richest and strongest" in its natural advantages. "Its population was a race of shepherds, as robust as they were simple and rude, and as brave as they were ignorant and uncivilized."

After visiting Nantes, Beltrami traveled up the Loire Valley, the "Garden of France" of the chateau-building kings. Angers, Saumur, Tours, Amboise, Blois, and Orleans engaged his interest, and the journey took two and a half months. Beltrami reached Paris at dark on February 28, 1822, after a tiresome coach ride, made uncomfortable by bad roads and disagreeable by the presence of two women whose "forwardness of . . . manners" disgusted him.

Beltrami, who had visited Paris twice before, had been absent from the city for more than fifteen years. Now he was pleasantly surprised at many changes in the city. He "found magnificent buildings where [he] had left miserable cottages; fine bridges and canals, which before did not exist; large streets and cheerful galleries where alleys ... formerly rendered the way dirty and dangerous.... Philosophy, munificence, and grandeur of design, are all equally conspicuous in the construction of the sewers, by means of which Paris is freed from the noxious exhalations which infected it."

Determined to observe the French character in Paris, Beltrami studiously avoided what he called "good society" but rather chose to frequent the *guinguettes* (cabarets), "where wine and gaiety draw out the natural language of the mind, and shew the heart in all its nakedness; where the French talk a great deal, but do not get drunk." Beltrami's objections to consorting with "good society" are character-revealing. At large parties, he said, "the exotic is confounded with the indigenous, the little with the great, the knave with the honest man, the spy with the minister; and dissimulation and flattery veil and disguise both persons and things."

Beltrami saw and did what tourists to Paris before and after him saw and did. He found Les Halles, the famous markets, rich in material for "the poet and the philosopher, the moralist and the politician, the architect and the painter." He attended the theater, "where the public does not sit in judgment on the actors, but the actors on the public." He visited the Chamber of Deputies, "where the interests and welfare of the public serve as a pretext to the adherents of old and pernicious institutions, to gratify their private enmities, and to pursue their private advantage."

The Italian's comments on the churches of Paris reflect his long-time hostility to the Jesuits. "True to their character of mortal enemies of kings and of people, [they] sow tares and discord, instead of preaching the morality and peace of the gospel," he wrote. He strolled through the famous Père La Chaise Cemetery, "most congenial to the present frame of my mind," but was shocked to find that "hatred and malignity have pursued their victims even in the grave," when he discovered that a monument to Marshal Michel Ney, *brave des braves*, erected by his wife and children, had been torn away by "the hand of power." Nevertheless, he added, "history cannot be silenced or obliterated." Beltrami deplored that the cemetery bore the "odious name . . . of the author of the decree for the revocation of the Edict of Nantes."

He made many excursions into the suburbs of Paris for relief from "the bustle and the disgusting gaiety of the Tuileries," and even went to "monotonous Versailles, because one must go to see it." Before he left Paris, one of his excursions took him to Ermenonville, where Jean-Jacques Rousseau lived and died.

If the face of Paris had changed since his last visit, its vices and pleasures remained unchanged, Beltrami noted: "Men still ruin themselves and descend to the lowest depths of vice in the gambling houses. . . . spies still haunt you at every step, . . . politics are still discussed at the shoeblack's as well as in the *salons*." But during his stay of two months the city presented "many agreeable surprises," and he concluded that "Paris, take it all in all, is still the metropolis of the world."

Next he traveled in easy stages to Strasbourg, where the spirit of tolerance delighted him. He found Catholics and Calvinists worshiping under the same roof in some churches which were divided by partition walls. "I felt my heart warmed with equal sympathy towards Catholics and Protestants," he wrote. "Would that it might produce the same effect on the hearts of the Jesuits!"

Crossing the Rhine at Strasbourg, Beltrami traveled extensively in Germany, visiting Baden-Baden, Karlsruhe, Mannheim, Heidelberg, Frankfurt, Mainz, Koblenz, Ems, Bonn, and Cologne before moving into the Low Countries. He found the Germans "obliging, and often truly and sincerely polite," the scenery lovely, and the wines delectable. He was profoundly impressed by a "revolution in surgery," which a Dr. Walcher of Bonn had achieved. "I was . . . taken to see a woman for whom he had made a new nose, after the original one had been entirely corroded by cancer," he wrote. "The piece of flesh with which he performed this extraordinary operation was taken out of her right arm. It is really a wonder of art . . . Surely after this Dr Walcher deserves a temple more than ever Esculapius did."

At Aachen, Beltrami found the tomb of Charlemagne as "simple and unpretending" as the emperor had been "heroic and illustrious." Louvain, he discovered, had "a great university without students, a great canal without commerce, and a great cathedral without a steeple or a bishop." In Brussels, his primary interest was Waterloo and he hastened out to the battlefield, where Wellington's victory and Napoleon's defeat "shook the whole world, and still influences the opinions and passions which agitate the two hemispheres." Beltrami philosophized, "The partisans of Napoleon still console themselves with the *ifs* and *buts*; but fate admits of no *ifs* or *buts*; the career of this extraordinary man was closed,—and he fell. Fate decreed that Toulon should be the cradle of his extraordinary political and military renown, and Waterloo its grave. . . . but glory . . . will be his to the end of time."

He visited Antwerp, where he was impressed by Napoleon's fortifications, docks, quays, and arsenals and by the "incomparable" paintings of Rubens. He moved on to Ghent, Bruges, and Ostende, which, he said, but for dikes built by Napoleon, "would have been swallowed up by the ocean." At Ostende, Beltrami took passage on a British packet for London, where after a twenty-six hour voyage he landed on July 10, 1822. "The stately Thames" fascinated him, as did London "in all its majesty, in all its grandeur," with "the numerous ships, steam vessels, and vessels of every size and form, some sailing up, and others down; . . . the arsenals and docks which animate its banks; . . . the vast floating forest of innumerable masts, . . . rising above the dark smoke that covers London as with a perpetual veil."

CHAPTER FOUR

"Bewildered in the Chaos"

"THE ENGLISH LANGUAGE . . . PREsents almost insurmountable barriers to the acquisition of any knowledge of the country," wrote Beltrami after two months in London, "bewildered in the chaos" of the great city. His frustration with the English language was wittily expressed:

> When we have learnt a little of it on the continent, we think we know enough for the necessary intercourse of life; we read it, and we fancy we understand it; we come here, hear it spoken, and . . . we cannot understand a single word. If you speak it as you read it, it is a charming jargon; your mouth and eyes are thrown into the most beautiful grimaces; every limb of your body is convulsed in the struggle to pronounce all these consonants, these strings of monosyllables. You give utterance to sounds which come from your stomach like volcanic eructations, shaking your whole frame like an electric shock, and, by sympathy, those of all who have the patience to listen to you.[1]

It was not only the language that baffled Beltrami in England. He found that footmen looked like lords and dukes like servants.

He went to the House of Commons expecting to see the pomp and trappings of state and instead found that members of Parliament were "very plain-looking men." And, unlike the ministers on the Continent with "the embroidered suits, the orders, the haughtiness, the stately repulsive air," the English ministers, "often the arbiters of both hemispheres, are not distinguishable from the other members of parliament, either by their seats, their dress, or their manners." Large palaces he found occupied by commoners while "small obscure-looking houses . . . are the residences of the king, or of a prince of the blood." He summed up his bewilderment: "I see the universe around me, and yet in no place on earth, not in the most secluded cottage in Italy, is one so solitary, so isolated, as in London. I fancy I see the most perfect uniformity, but I find the most astonishing contrasts. . . . How can I give . . . even the slightest idea of this extraordinary country?" [2]

The tourist in Beltrami broke through the confusion and he set forth to see the sights with his accustomed enthusiastic curiosity. He characterized London as "vast rather than grand"; it was not a city but "a province covered with buildings." Like the English gardens, London has "something of everything in it; it is the favourite empire of variety and of caprice, and there is space for the display of all." [3]

Beltrami, still using Napoleon as a measuring rod, said that London's bridges of stone or iron had no rivals in the world except those that Bonaparte had built at Paris and Bordeaux. He found Waterloo bridge "imposing and magnificent," although "too heavy," and he was interested in the mechanism which recorded each foot-passenger who paid a penny to cross the bridge. The device, he said, "registers the number of passengers in a day, and operates as an effectual check on the cupidity of any toll receiver who might be tempted to betray his trust. I point out this little circumstance, to shew . . . to what a pitch of refinement the industry, the genius for creating and the talent for controlling mechanical operations, are pushed in this country." [4]

English houses, wrote the traveler, were more comfortable than those in Italy and greater attention was paid there to cleanliness. The London parks were more fields than parks and "cows take the precedency of all competitors . . . but happily the English cows forget they have horns, and do not assume the right of walking about the streets, and marching into the coffee-houses, as the goats do at Rome." Beltrami praised the English good taste in leaving the parks in a natural state, deeming it unnecessary "to torture and mangle nature as the French and Italians do, to force her into regularities which she abhors." [5]

Westminster Abbey, "the finest specimen of Gothic architecture in London, and one of the most ancient in Christendom . . . is not inferior to the best we have in Italy, or to any of those we have seen in France, or the Low Countries," Beltrami declared. He was surprised to find "the unfortunate Mary Stuart" buried in the same chapel as "her rival and murderer Elizabeth." He was disappointed to find in England, "a philosophical and judicious country," so many memorials to unworthy persons: "There are an abundance of great monuments of little kings; and, as elsewhere, epitaphs which exalt to the skies men whom the Creator called into existence only to scourge the earth; men whose bodies the posthumous judgments of Egypt would have condemned to the birds of prey, rather than to honourable sepulture." [6]

One day, when his excursion led him to a large tavern with gardens, he witnessed "a sight *entirely new,* and somewhat strange . . . a boxing-match." When two young men exchanged defiant words, and then left, each accompanied by friends, Beltrami departed too. "Curious as I am to see everything," he wrote, "it was in my vocation to follow them, which I did. Not seeing any arms, I thought I had gone in vain; but I soon perceived that it was by blows with the fist that the vanquished was to be overthrown, and the conqueror crowned." Beltrami's "ringside report" is interesting:

> The most perfect quiet prevailed over the voices and countenances of the numerous spectators of the combat; nothing was heard but the fall of the tremendous blows; and I perceived that my astonishment and the feelings which I could not conceal at the sight of these disfigured countenances, which every blow rendered more terrible, was regarded as indecorous and offensive. The seconds stopped them, from time to time, to give them rest and recruit their strength, after which they set them on as they would have done bull dogs, yet without the slightest change in their immovable manner, or profound silence. . . . And are we less barbarous, who, like butchers, slaughter each other at the altar of honour? [7]

Beltrami's eye for beauty, quite naturally, extended to the women into whose presence his social excursion brought him. In England, he wrote with extravagant gallantry, "one meets with physiognomies . . . which bear the impress of divinity," and he expatiated on "that delicate complexion, that alabaster skin, that small mouth, those rosy lips, those dove-like eyes . . . It is certainly true that England possesses a great number of pretty women." Beltrami was impressed by "their modest and timid air." This, he asserted, "when it does not amount to coldness,—which it too often does—renders them yet more interesting."

The dress of English women, the Italian found to be "elegant, and exquisitely neat;" but he felt that it would be yet more becoming to them "if it were less varied as to colour, and more light, less rich and more simple." Beltrami expressed his admiration for English women "more in *déshabillé* than in full dress."

Beltrami held forth at some length on the attainments, both intellectual and physical, of English women:

> The education of Englishwomen is carried to a high pitch; nowhere are women so well informed. They also shine with a thousand subordinate accomplishments—too many perhaps; so that in general they are profound in nothing. The thing in which they excel all other women is equitation. They ride much better than the men, who, in my opinion, have no very knightly or equestrian air with their *saliscendi* or peculiar way of rising in the stirrup. If this tends to spare fatigue, as they say, it may be very well to adopt it on a long journey; but, for a ride in town, it seems to me as useless as it is graceless and abrupt. They also surpass the men in all the qualities which distinguish the social being: their manners are infinitely better, and, in general, science apart, they are as well informed as the men.

The Italian deliberately avoided any attempt to discover whether English women were more or less discreet than those of his native land. He wrote: "This is too delicate a point, and one nowise within the competency of a rambler, still less one of my principles . . . moreover, I abhor all those odious and invidious comparisons. . . . English women are very prudent;—and that is great praise; for weakness is human, prudence divine."

Beltrami capsuled his comparison of the women of England with those of France and Italy "by heartily agreeing that what has been said by somebody, that a French woman is best for gallantry, an Italian for love and friendship, and an Englishwoman for household duties."

Fashionable society, to which Beltrami had entry, interested the observant Italian because, "although composed of the same elements as that of other nations," it was different from any in which he had moved. He was attracted by the "air of affability" which usually prevailed and the "ease of manner bordering on quiet nonchalance" with which English people of fashion demonstrated their "superiority to forms and civilities." He concluded that this trait was based more on pride than liberality, because, he said, Englishmen of all degree believe conformity to rules of politeness to be humiliating. At one affair he attended, the Danish Prince Royal "received no more respect than such an obscure individual as myself."

Beltrami was introduced into club life in London and his defense of this famous British institution suggests that his ego was flattered by his membership in the Travellers' Club which, with a trace of snobbery, he described as having "a most distinguished rank." Clubs, he said, were indispensable in a country like England. In the streets, Englishmen must be "obedient subjects to the sovereignty of the people," so the private clubs were necessary "to preserve the state of society from a debasing mixture" by separating "well-educated and well-bred people from those who are not so." Membership in the Travellers' Club was extended only to those who had traveled at least 500 miles in a direct line from England. Its roster, at the time Beltrami was admitted, included Arthur Wellesley, the Duke of Wellington, and four future prime ministers of Great Britain—Lord Aberdeen, George Canning, Lord John Russell, and Lord Palmerston. He described the clubs: "In these clubs everything is well conceived, and well arranged. All that regards the convenience and comfort of English life—all that order, decency, and dignity require, are there. The attendance is ready and precise, and the most *brilliant* cleanliness is united to solid elegance. There are rooms for study, where you find a choice library—all the newspapers, pamphlets, and periodical publications. There are other rooms for conversation. You find baths and dressing-rooms; and, if necessary, excellent cookery." [8]

England's freedom of the press and its resulting benefits to society greatly impressed Beltrami. Some journals denounced infringements on the people, others defended the royal prerogatives, and between them they "distinguished monarchy from republic and republic from monarchy . . . and oppose each other in order to prevent the harm each respectively might do." Writing more at length on English newspapers, Beltrami said:

> The newspapers and periodical works of England are equally the censors of licentiousness and of despotism. . . .
>
> Nothing escapes the English journalists. In England, therefore, people who read nothing but the newspapers may be well informed, or at least, may have a general idea of what is passing in the world; and this is no trifle. . . . [They] are the mirrors which reflect the progress of the human mind, the discoveries in science, philosophy, political economy, and literature. . . . they are . . . where the minds both of people and kings may find all that is requisite for private or for public life.[9]

As a jurist Beltrami was puzzled that the British continued their traditional legal system based on both common law and statutory law. "Why not give," he asks, "a uniform and harmonious character and course to the whole body of English laws, as Napoleon did to those of France, which were a perfect chaos?" British judges sat with due decorum but Beltrami thought Italian courts displayed more dignity than he had seen anywhere in his travels.

Beltrami was astonished to learn that in London alone,

"there are not fewer than *forty thousand* persons who live by law-suits and chicanery; and perhaps almost as many who subsist on prescriptions, calomel, blisters, etc."

It was natural that Beltrami should study the paradox of aristocracy and democracy, "these two great antagonizing powers of the social machine of England." Although he declared that he had never seen "an aristocracy more aristocratic than that of England," he hastened to point out that "every class in England is radically aristocratic." He noted that all segments of society reflected an "inveterate and habitual aristocracy of feeling and opinion." Even in the humblest of cottages, "every one takes the place assigned him by his respective class, and with a suitable deportment." He concluded that an English house, whether great or humble, was "the most venerated sanctuary of aristocracy," and the English people were "its most pious devotees." While an Englishman is "an aristocrat in his domestic circles," he is assuredly "a democrat amongst his fellow citizens." Beltrami felt that in public the Englishman was more democratic than he was aristocratic in private. "I have been treated with a degree of haughty reserve, in a house, by a man who offered me his arm as soon as he quitted it," he wrote.

Beltrami's comments on religion in England, with its multiplicity of sects, are frequently punctuated by his recurring caustic criticism of the Jesuits. Beltrami's bias against the religious order as well as his admiration for Napoleon repeatedly intrude into his narrative. In a day when anti-Semitism was widespread, Beltrami, although annoyed by the importunities of a peddler who wished to buy his old clothes—"the Jews of London call all clothes from the continent *old clothes*," he said—showed unusual sympathy for Jews: "I am lost in astonishment when I think of this scattered and yet powerful people, and of the prejudices concerning them by which we are blinded." [10]

The Italian, of course, did not spend all his time in London, but ventured into the nearby countryside and visited Oxford, Birmingham, and Chester before he reached Liverpool, from where he intended to sail for America. As he traveled, Beltrami acquired a deeper understanding of English manners and English character. These, he said, were well exemplified by the legendary John Bull:

> He is an animal who, like the bull, naturally stiff, clumsy and tranquil, becomes active, light and ferocious, when irritated; like him, he is constant in his habits and obstinate in his temper; like him, laborious, and neither fiery nor indolent. He plants himself opposite to you, like his prototype, stares at you with no very kind expression; ruminates continually, and never explains himself. It is the perfectly English Englishman whom I have the honour to introduce in this fictitious personage; or at least this is, I think, what the English mean when they talk of John Bull. . . .
>
> The unsophisticated John Bull, like many others, is never satisfied with the present, he always looks back to "the good old times." . . . In his *home*, and in all that depends upon him, his habits are his sublunary divinities. . . . He thinks himself prodigiously cunning, and he is very distrustful; but he is easily duped by anybody who will talk his language, adopt his habits and prejudices. He always thinks he is right, and he is often wrong; but to convince him of this is not an easy task. He is always abusing the government, England, and the English; but, on emergency, he would give all he is worth in the world for the glory of the government, England, and the English. He is irascible and violent, but rarely vindictive. . . . He is a Tory from habit, a Whig from inclination; an aristocrat from vanity, a democrat from principle. . . .
>
> . . . English he is and English he will be.[11]

That Beltrami had made a shrewd, witty analysis of the British character, is evidenced by the comments of the British press on the publication of the English edition of his book in 1828. The *Scots Times* declared, "It is not often that a foreigner at once hits upon the strong points and appreciates the many seeming contradictions of our national character. . . . Mr. Beltrami even in his short stay has done so." To the *Quarterly Review*, "M. Beltrami's observations on London and the manners of the English generally are more correct than foreigners are apt to make." [12]

On this point, another of Beltrami's estimates of the British is not inappropriate: "The English are like artichokes, you must strip off a great many leaves before you lay them bare. . ." [13]

Beltrami sailed from Liverpool on the ship *Reaper* on October 25, 1822. He had intended to sail to New York on a "comfortable" packet, but when he learned that yellow fever was prevalent there, he changed his plans and took passage for Philadelphia. It was, he recorded, a miserable voyage, with insufficient supplies and an inadequate crew. To add to the discomfort, Beltrami was ill—severely at times—during the stormy crossing, which took sixty days. Beltrami's provisions, including a stock of fine wines, liquors, and a medicine chest, became common property of crew and passengers, who took advantage of his illness. Indeed he was so ill that at one time he was given little chance to recover. Reduced to a daily ration of boiled rice, the passengers faced malnutrition on the voyage. Only Beltrami's strong constitution and a will to survive prevailed against ailments and elements. Finally, the battered ship arrived at Philadelphia on December 30, 1822.[14] Notwithstanding the discomforts and hardships of the voyage and his long sickness, Beltrami could not help but note the ability of the captain and the crew throughout three furious Atlantic storms. Beltrami concluded that American seamen would make their country "one of the most formidable maritime powers of the world." [15]

Pondering his reasons for visiting America, he had written, "I ask you . . . why I should stagnate in London or Paris. . . . What is to be gained by travelling in Europe, where everything is antiquated and despotic? . . . The sight and the study of people, in whom the virtues which enabled them to triumph over European oppression are yet in all their freshness, are best calculated to fill the mind with useful ideas, and to form the heart to philosophy and resignation." [16]

And so Giacomo Costantino Beltrami, at the age of forty-three, had fared forth on a voyage, which, far from his thoughts at the time, would take him into the wilds of North America.

CHAPTER FIVE

"I Am the President"

THE DOOR OF THE PRESIDENT'S house was open and unattended, and Giacomo Beltrami entered. Armed with a letter of introduction to James Monroe he looked in vain for someone of whom he could make inquiry. Opposite the vestibule he saw an open door and crossing to it, he entered another room, calling out for permission to enter, but there was no response. After he had called out several times, a man appeared. To Beltrami, he seemed "old." He wore leather riding breeches and top boots with spurs. In his hand was a riding whip.

"Is the President at home?" inquired the Italian. Can I have the honour of seeing him?"

"You do see him," replied the man in boots. "I am the President, at your service." This sudden, unexpected confrontation with James Monroe left Beltrami, for the moment, speechless; but the President quickly put his visitor at ease and the Italian's embarrassment disappeared. After presenting his letter of introduction, Beltrami engaged Monroe in a long and amiable conversation. The visitor was profoundly impressed by the President's courtesy and kindness and, he wrote, he "quitted this illustrious chief magistrate with an impression of the deepest respect and veneration." [1]

Although Beltrami meticulously recorded what he saw and what he did, in the matter of dates he was careless. Accordingly, the date of his interview with President Monroe can be only approximated as sometime in mid-March, 1823. The Italian did not indicate what he and President Monroe discussed.

Before leaving for the American capital, Beltrami had spent his first days in America preparing his European travel notes for publication by a Philadelphia printer. He was unimpressed by Philadelphia as a place for "amiable or courteous manners," and found the upper class imbued with "illiberal and spiteful ambition." Yet he concluded during his stay in Philadelphia that among nations, the United States "is one of the most civilized, precisely because not over-civilized." He was impressed by the University of Pennsylvania, the public library, a philosophical society, the museum of natural history, and the city's hospitals and churches. He also noted the many public schools and concluded that "they build as many schools as churches." The Philadelphia markets "are really beautiful," he wrote, "and the quantity and excellence of the provisions, and game of every description, is a novel and striking sight to a stranger." Before leaving Philadelphia, Beltrami made almost $1,000 in purchases of articles from J. B. Tasca, a local merchant. Some of the purchases were shipped to Europe as gifts to friends upon his return. But Beltrami had shipped to him in New Orleans 500 copies of his book, six dozen umbrellas, twelve malacca canes and five other canes mounted in gold. These articles, Beltrami undoubtedly hoped to sell at a profit in New Orleans. At the same time, it is reasonable to assume that Beltrami may have purchased the large red umbrella which would serve him well during his

The "President's House" (the White House) about the time Beltrami called on President James Monroe.

then-unthought-of expedition into the wilderness. His thoughts were on visiting the seats of governments.

En route to Washington, Beltrami stopped at Baltimore, which he found "pretty and cheerful in all parts . . . perfectly brilliant with neatness." By this time he had occasion to record his first impression of American women: "They are generally pretty—at least their countenances are extremely interesting to me; they are agreeable without forwardness, modest without affectation, well-informed without pedantry; and are excellent housewives. In all respects, they are very superior to the men." [2]

After his visit with James Monroe in the White House, Beltrami explored Washington, which he called the "queen-city of America." His justification of this epithet is interesting: "the influence she exercises on this new world, already so astonishingly mature, seems to justify me even at this moment, and time will justify me yet more fully." The "vast" Capitol, situated so as to command the whole city, with a fine view of the White House, "might have been rendered grand," Beltrami mused, "if the . . . architect had not preferred the new to the regular;—if he had not thought extravagancies more striking than the rules of art, harmony too monotonous, and fantastic embellishments grand and magnificent." He objected to the grand staircase, "which rises majestically in the centre of the eastern façade," because he believed "so grand an edifice . . . ought to have had a majestic entrance, where carriages might have set down the members of congress at the foot of a grand interior staircase." Beltrami concluded that this was probably "too aristocratical an indulgence," so the architect made Congressmen "alight democratically in the rain." [3]

He visited the House of Representatives, "a magnificent room, in the form of a crescent," with Enrico Causici's statue of Liberty (a plaster model never executed) in a niche above the speaker's rostrum. The Senate chamber he found much smaller, but handsome, and the Supreme Court located in a "well-contrived, if not magnificent" room. He noted that the attorney general kept his breakfast in a little closet in the courtroom. To the amazement of the Italian visitor, the attorney general ate his breakfast "in very good earnest and without the slightest constraint, in full court and in the midst of the audience." [4]

While in Washington, Beltrami was angered by the cold reception he received from "a miserable French diplomatist" to whom he had a letter of introduction. He contrasted the Frenchman's brusqueness with President Monroe's "noble manners" and remarked the "difference between the frank and liberal tone of conversation of the one, and the pitiful inquisitiveness of the other." [5]

Shortly after his visit to the White House, Beltrami set out from Washington for Pittsburgh, where he planned to take passage on a steamboat for New Orleans. Traveling over a "detestable road," with the passengers "packed like red herrings, in a bad stage-coach," the cultured Italian found his fellow travelers to be Kentuckians, "whom it is really impossible to endure. It is a pity that a people so brave, industrious, and active, should be so coarse and insolent," he wrote. "One can and must esteem them, but it is a difficult matter to like them."

To get away from such crowded quarters, he left the stagecoach at Frederick, Maryland and hired a wagon. Continuing over the mountains to Pittsburgh, he was fascinated by the diversified country through which he passed—"forests, *prairies*, tilled fields, plains, hills, vallies [sic], mountains, rivers, and torrents"—and villages and towns that are "the seat of the greatest prosperity and the most perfect and solid liberty." "There is no room for monotony," he wrote, because of the "boundless variety"

The United States Capitol, which Beltrami found lacked "a majestic entrance, where carriages might have set down the members of Congress at the foot of a grand interior staircase."

everywhere apparent. To the traveler from Italy, it was "one continuous gallery of the finest pictures from the hand of Nature." [6]

Noting that fifty years earlier, Americans had considered Pittsburgh the end of the civilized world, he found the city had become "the little Birmingham of the United States," with a flourishing iron foundry and steam-powered factories "all in great activity." Insatiably curious, Beltrami closely observed a machine that manufactured nails. "So powerful is the mechanism . . . that, with my watch in my hand, I have seen more than three hundred made in a minute [by] one man," Beltrami wrote. Almost a century and a half before air pollution became a national concern in the United States, Beltrami commented upon its presence in Pittsburgh: "The coal-smoke, the only incense which the manufacturing and heretical inhabitants offer to their two divinities, Avarice and Industry, enshrouds the sun by day and the stars by night." [7]

Beltrami reached Pittsburgh late in March, 1823, and booked passage on a steamboat for the confluence of the Ohio and Mississippi rivers, where he expected to take the packet *United States* down the Mississippi to New Orleans. He began his journey down the Ohio on April 1, and he found much to capture his interest in the ten-day voyage. Although he protested that "neither time nor my pen would suffice to describe . . . all the impressions which the different aspects of this magnificent river produce upon the mind," he proceeded to record many pages of these impressions.

The Italian traveler found on the steamboats "every possible accommodation, . . . a tolerable degree of neatness," and meals that were "plain but plentiful." To his bed, Beltrami said, the "noise of the water and the machinery imparts a soporific virtue not to be found elsewhere." The bridges along the way he considered "beautiful proofs of the progress of mechanism among the Americans," especially the two at Pittsburgh, built entirely of wood and resting upon stone pillars. "Each of these bridges has a *trottoir* on both sides, where foot-passengers cannot be incommoded by the horses or carriages, for which there are separate entrances; they are like spacious galleries which afford a shelter from the wind and rain."

The infant city of Cincinnati, he thought, promised much. He called it a miniature Genoa, and found it full of activity and industry. He was surprised to find at an academy of five hundred scholars that the girls were mixed with the boys. This prompted him to philosophize, "Notwithstanding the respect due to the morals of the Americans, one cannot help fearing that opportunity will prevail over the most austere principles. There may be the most primitive simplicity and purity, but nature speaks a still more seducing language than the corruptions of society."

After the steamboat passed the Miami River, which Beltrami noted emptied into the Ohio about four hundred and seventy miles from Pittsburgh, the Italian traveler was fascinated by the small village of Rising Sun which stood on a small hill on the Indiana side of the river. "Its brilliant beauty and picturesque situation perfectly justify its name," he observed. But Beltrami reserved a greater enthusiasm for the little town of Vevay, Indiana. He wrote: "This little town, although in the bosom of America, is like the *Pays de Vaud,* inhabited by Swiss who are very successful agriculturists. . . . These Swiss cultivate the vine: they are the only settlers who have hitherto had any success in this branch of agriculture."

The Falls of the Ohio, of which he had heard so much,

proved a great disappointment to Beltrami. Following his usual practice of not asking questions about works of art or works of nature in advance, he made no inquiries about the cascades. (He said that he preferred "a surprise either more agreeable or more intense" and that he wanted, at any rate, his eyes and judgment to "be under the influence of no other impressions than their own"). The Italian did not disguise his reaction to the Falls of the Ohio: "But here my expectations, raised by the idea of the fall of so large a volume of water, were grievously disappointed; and my only astonishment was, that there was nothing to be astonished at." Continuing, Beltrami said:

> These falls are nothing more than an inclined plane of only twenty-two feet in the space of two miles; which in fact produces no other effect than that of rendering the current more rapid. I observed, however, a phenomenon which appears extraordinary.
>
> I thought that the velocity impressed upon such a volume of water by this descent, must have given it an irresistible force, and have accelerated the current to a considerable distance; but this was not the fact; the river, at the bottom of this inclined plane, immediately resumes, as if by magic, its level and its ordinary rapidity, without the least reflux. We . . . must leave the solution of this problem to the learned.

Noting that Louisville, Kentucky, was a thriving town of 8,000 population, Beltrami expressed surprise at its size, considering that "a great number of the inhabitants yearly fall a sacrifice to the pestilential exhalations of the surrounding marshes, as well as the contradictory systems of the swarm of medical men by whom it is infested."

As the steamboat passed Wilkinsonville, named for

General James Wilkinson, Beltrami recorded some of the high spots of the Aaron Burr affair, in which Wilkinson was an actor. When the vessel put in for a cargo of flour at a place which, "although it contains only two cats and a chimney, is called *America*," Beltrami utilized the time to explore the woods, "the attractions of which I can never resist."

Accompanied by a fellow passenger, Beltrami struck off into the "primeval forests [which] are extremely inviting to a man born in the midst of the gardens of the beautiful but over-cultivated Hesperia."

Beltrami said that the pair returned with "a stock of laughter which lasted us and the company for a long time." His description of the incident is amusing:

> I was behind a large oak watching a squirrel, when suddenly my companion called out, "A deer!" I asked where? He replied, "Upon a tree." Wishing to return the jest, I desired him to get some bird-lime and catch it, like a beccafigo; but seeing that he actually believed what he wished *me* to believe, I suspected there was some strange blunder; I therefore approached it:—it was a panther! I cannot tell which became the paler of the two, but certainly the face of my American friend was not blooming. Our guns were loaded with small-shot, so that to fire would only have been to irritate her. We were perfectly agreed as to the propriety of not disturbing her, since she was so obliging as not to stir. We retired, and, borne upon the wings of fear, with the sun for our compass, we soon reached our steamboat, though we had plunged into a very thick, pathless forest.
>
> We immediately returned to the spot, accompanied by some huntsmen of the village, and better armed; but the animal was gone.
>
> When we first saw her she was carelessly lying upon the junction of two large arms of one of those venerable

> maples which still abound in these regions. There are a great many panthers in these immense forests: they remain thus motionless upon the trees that they may more easily fall upon the squirrels which abound there, and which are their favorite food.

In due time, the boat reached the mouth, where the Ohio joined the Mississippi. The passengers disembarked at a large log house built upon piles on the edge of the river. This served as an inn for travelers awaiting steamboats going up the Mississippi to St. Louis or down the river to New Orleans. There Beltrami established himself. He had several days, while awaiting the *United States*, to contemplate the meeting place of the Ohio and the Mississippi rivers. "The current of these two rivers is, as it were, paralyzed for about twenty miles above their confluence, which seems to show that the volume of the Ohio is as powerful at this place as that of the Mississippi," Beltrami wrote.

The junction of the two great rivers, Beltrami declared, "is one of the greatest spectacles of nature," but he confessed that he was baffled by the sight. He wrote: ". . . the theories of gravitation and pressure, of attraction and repulsion, of inclination and equilibrium,—in short, all that concerns the general laws of the motion of fluids, —here offer a vast field of battle to the learned in hydraulics, hydrometrics, hydrostatics, hydrodynamics, and a whole dictionary of such hard words, I give place to them; for all this is worse than Greek to me."

About mid-April a steamboat appeared in the distance and Beltrami prepared to embark for New Orleans. But the vessel was not the southbound *United States*. It was the *Calhoun*, heading for St. Louis. On board were Major Lawrence Taliaferro, the Indian agent at Fort St. Anthony, and General William Clark, superintendent for Indian affairs at St. Louis, who were returning to their posts after a trip to Washington. A meeting with these two American officers changed the destiny of Giacomo Costantino Beltrami and transformed him from a casual traveler over established routes into a pioneer explorer of the Northwest wilderness.[8]

CHAPTER SIX

River of Vast Extent

THE INNATE CURIOSITY OF BELtrami led him into conversation with Clark and Taliaferro, and when he learned the nature of their mission, his lively imagination was stimulated. He besieged them with questions about the Indians, their habits, customs, rituals, daily life. Years later, the major recalled Beltrami's absorption: "To learn the habits of the Indian tribes was almost a mania with him," [1] he wrote. Beltrami himself described his growing excitement in learning more of the American red man: "The descriptions I had read of their extraordinary character had, from infancy, excited both my astonishment and my incredulity; what these gentlemen had the goodness to communicate justified both, and re-awakened a curiosity which I had always intended to gratify before my departure from America: never could a better opportunity arise, nor could anything, I thought, be more interesting to a foreigner; I therefore determined to accompany them."

And so, instead of waiting for the *United States* to take him down the river to New Orleans, he took passage on the *Calhoun* for St. Louis and began the ascent of the "river of vast extent, of a majesty which it is difficult to conceive." The *Calhoun* pushed out into the channel of the Mississippi in a torrential April rain. Captivated by "the grand and terrific scenery . . . truly magical, imposing, and novel," Beltrami sat on the deck, undeterred by the downpour.[2]

During the three-day voyage to St. Louis, Beltrami and Major Taliaferro[3] developed a mutual cordiality. Their common origin—for Taliaferro's ancestors were Italians from Genoa who had reached Jamestown in 1637—provided a basis for pleasant relations. At every opportunity, Beltrami plied Taliaferro with questions about the Indians; and at times chided him for dropping the *g* from his name (the Italian form was *Tagliaferro*). The major found Beltrami's presence and manner highly agreeable and his mind stimulating. Years later, he described the Italian's "commanding appearance . . . proud of bearing, and quick of temper, high spirited, but always the gentleman."[4]

As the *Calhoun* steamed upstream, Beltrami determined to visit the Indian tribes. He was, however, somewhat taken aback by the first Indians that he saw at St. Louis. "I was surprised at their grotesque appearance," he wrote. "I hope soon to see them more closely, and to observe the workings of their minds and the habits of their lives."

The St. Louis where Beltrami remained for a few days was a town of 7,000 French, Spanish, American, and Canadian inhabitants. Because of "this assemblage of various nations," Beltrami found St. Louis society "less cold and formal than in purely American towns." The attractive and fashionable women at a brilliant ball made him forget that the city was "on the threshold of savage life."[5]

On April 21, the steamboat *Virginia* left St. Louis with Major Taliaferro and Beltrami aboard, bound for Fort

Major Lawrence Taliaferro—As U. S. Agent at Fort Snelling for the Sioux and Chippewa Indian Tribes, Taliaferro greatly assisted Beltrami in his expedition into the wilds of Minnesota. (Courtesy Minnesota Historical Society).

St. Anthony.[6] In Beltrami's opinion, this voyage was "an epoch in the history of navigation . . . an enterprise of the boldest, of the most extraordinary nature, and probably unparalleled." Never before had a steamboat ascended so far—"twenty-two thousand miles" [sic][7]—above the mouth of the river. The voyage of the *Virginia* to Fort St. Anthony was indeed a significant pioneer venture because it demonstrated the practicability of navigation on the Upper Mississippi River. Beltrami quite properly considered himself a participant in a history-making voyage and his superlatives were not misplaced.

The *Virginia,* built in Wheeling in 1819, was owned by a syndicate headed by Redick McKee and James Pemberton. It was Pemberton who acted as captain part of the time on the historic voyage of the 118-foot stern-wheeler of 109.32 tons. The captain's name, the Italian wrote, "deserves to be proclaimed by one of the hundred mouths of Fame. He is justly entitled to the admiration of mankind, the gratitude of his fellow-citizens, and of his government." Ironically, Beltrami himself gave Pemberton's name incorrectly—as "Perston."

As the *Virginia* pursued its uncharted course up "the river of vast extent," the Italian traveler enjoyed the excitement and novelty of the voyage. One incident that astonished Beltrami involved Great Eagle, a chief of the tribe of Saukis. General Clark persuaded the chief to leave his canoe with his tribesmen and join Major Taliaferro's party. Clark had presented the chief with a handsome military uniform, which with deference Great Eagle put on for the departure. Beltrami related the sequel: "The first thing he did, when we were some distance from shore, was to take off the uniform which had been given him . . . as a present from the *Great Father,* (the name used by the savages to designate the president of the United States.) He shewed great satisfaction at finding himself once more in *statu quo* of our first parents. The youngest of his two children had not even a fig-leaf, or a bit of cloth round the loins, whilst we were shivering with cold, though wrapped in our winter flannel and great coats."

The chief provided Beltrami with his first insight into the character of the Indians in another amusing incident. "The Great Eagle, vexed and angry that the pilot had not taken his advice respecting the choice of the channel [the *Virginia* had run aground on a sandbar], jumped into the river and swam to the western bank, whence he spoke to his children [who remained on the boat]; and disdaining to remain any longer in the steam-boat, returned home, that is to say, into the forest."

The next day, the *Virginia* reached Fort Edwards, situated about 220 miles above St. Louis. Awaiting its arrival was Great Eagle, surrounded by his tribe, in a temporary encampment on the shore. Hardly had the encampment come into their sight when the chief's two children plunged into the river and, said Beltrami, "swam to their den with all the eagerness of wild beasts escaping from a menagerie into their native forests."

When the *Virginia* tied up, Great Eagle came aboard to secure his bow, quiver, and gun. Beltrami was delighted when the Indian, who remained exasperated and resentful toward the pilot and the steamboat's company, put out his hand as a mark of friendship to the Italian. Beltrami seized this favorable moment to ask Great Eagle for the gift of a scalp hanging from his tomahawk. The scalp was that of a Sioux chief whom Great Eagle had killed in combat. "Savages have no control over the impulse of the moment," mused Beltrami, "and as the Great Eagle was now as much softened as he had been the day before irritated, he could not refuse my request."

Beltrami had adventures of his own on the voyage.

Water color by Seth Eastman (Courtesy Hill Reference Library, St. Paul).

Water color by Peter Rindisbacher in the United States Military Academy, West Point, New York.

How the Indian traveled is shown in these pictures of the Sioux (above) traveling in summer and the Chippewa traveling in winter. Beltrami was astounded at the way the women were used almost as beasts of burden.

Once the Italian wandered into the forest while the *Virginia* tied up to take on fuel wood. Attracted by the woodland and by a flock of wild turkeys which his steps surprised, he ventured far into the forest. Suddenly, to his dismay, he realized he was lost.

Using his compass, he finally arrived at the place where he had left the *Virginia*; but the steamboat was gone! He discharged his gun, but the shots "resounded vainly in the forest." He turned then, to his last resort—his legs. "But the speed of Atalanta would have been useless among the brushwood and the ruins of *pre-adamite* trees," he wrote. Fortunately, while Beltrami stumbled about, panic rising in him, the steamboat ran onto a sandbar. It was then that his absence from the *Virginia* was noted, and a canoe was dispatched to search for him. It arrived, wrote Beltrami, "just in time, for I was so completely out of breath that I must have given up the pursuit." Shortly after his return to the *Virginia*, it was afloat again and the voyage continued.

Because of the swiftness of the current, the trip up the river from Fort Edwards was full of difficulties. The *Virginia* once had to turn back because it was too heavily laden to navigate the rapids. Beltrami made extensive notes on the Indians he sighted, and on the meadows, groves, and forests just beginning to show green. "Never had I seen nature more beautiful, more majestic, than in this vast domain of silence and solitude," he wrote. "Every object was as new to my imagination as to my eye."

When the *Virginia* tied up near an encampment of Saukis at the mouth of the Rocky River, Beltrami eagerly went ashore to visit among the Indians. Their habitations, he found, were nothing more than "huts . . . covered with mats or skins." Elliptical in shape, with a round opening in the center of the roof for smoke to escape, these huts sheltered, noted the Italian, "a family, sometimes two, with or without their relations. They sleep in a circle upon skins, mats, or dried grass."

Mealtime among the Saukis was particularly interesting to Beltrami:

> A copper or tin boiler which they get in exchange from the traders, often supported only by a wooden fork stuck in the ground, pieces of wood hollowed into spoons, bits of the bark of trees formed into plates and dishes, the horns of buffalos or other animals cut into cups, constitute the whole of their *batterie de cuisine,* their plate, and their table service. A stake supplies the place of a spit, their fingers serve for forks, the earth for a table, and a skin or the beautiful carpet of nature for their table-cloth.
>
> They all sit indiscriminately around the food with which Providence and their guns supply them. Neither kings, ministers, nor courtiers are treated with any distinction.
>
> In this perfect republic, equality is not less the privilege of animals than men. The dogs, although *illegitimate* and descended from wolves, are seated at the same table with the savages, and at the same *divan;* they partake of the same dishes, and sleep on the same beds. I have seen young bears and otters treated as a part of the community.

Although the Saukis' features were "characteristic of their savage state," they were not, stated the Italian, "disagreeable." Their heads were "rather small," and generally without hair "except a small tuft . . . like that of the Turks; this gives the forehead an appearance of great elevation." They have small eyes and thin eyebrows, Beltrami noted, and the cornea approached to yellow, the pupils to red. Continuing his description of the physical appearance of the Saukis, Beltrami wrote:

> Their ears are sufficiently large to bear all the jewels, &c. with which they are adorned: . . . I have seen . . . bells, heads of birds and dozens of buckles, which penetrated the whole cartilaginous part from top to bottom. Their noses are large and flat, like those of the nations of eastern Asia; their nostrils are pierced and ornamented like their ears. The maxillary bones, *or pomettes,* are very prominent. The under jaw extends outwards on both sides. Their mouths are rather large, their teeth close set, and of the finest enamel; their lips a little inverted. Their necks are regularly formed: they have large bellies and narrow chests, so that their bodies are generally larger below than above. Their feet and hands are well proportioned; their arms are slender: . . . the legs, . . . are more robust than the rest of their frame. Their complexion is copper-coloured, whence they call themselves the *red people,* . . . they have no hair on any part of the body.

What astonished Beltrami about the Indians was the scantiness of their attire even during bitter cold weather. "They wear a covering around the loins," he said. "All the rest of the body, even the head, is naked, whether it rains, hails or freezes, or the earth is parched with the burning heat of the dog-days."

Beltrami was particularly interested in the lot of the Indian women, who, he soon noted, "are the porters, the beasts of burden of the men." They wear a short tunic with large sleeves and with plates of white metal covering the breast. A close-fitting petticoat reached below the knees. In winter their feet and legs were covered, but in summer they are uncovered.

Noting that the Indian women in their youth have attractive forms, Beltrami observed that "these flowers soon fade: the evening succeeds to the morning without the interval of noon." Continuing, the Italian wrote:

> There is no slavery more abject than that of the Indian women. They are looked upon with such contempt, that

> the greatest insult to an Indian is to say to him, "Go, you are a *squaw*." It frequently happens that these victims of the instinctive tyranny of man have such a horror of the fate of their sex, that they destroy their daughters at birth, to save them from the wretched, miserable life which awaits them.

Beltrami noted a strange custom among the Saukis. Normally, "the men and women daub their faces with red, yellow, white, or blue. When they are in mourning they paint the whole face, and even the body, black, during a year; the second year, they paint only half; and, at last, merely streak themselves with it in various patterns."

Beltrami had an opportunity to observe a medicine dance, which he described as "the offspring of political knavery and superstitious folly and credulity."

He was surprised when he saw, for the first time, the dexterity with which the Indians handle their bows. "Children, nine or ten years of age, hit a small piece of money . . . which I had fixed up for them to aim at, at a distance of twenty-five paces,—often at the second trial," he wrote. "At last I was obliged to remove it to thirty-five, or they would soon have exhausted the little purse I had filled for this visit." [8]

The Indians, Beltrami said, had heard only of the French, English, Spaniards, and Americans, and their conception of the outside world was confined to these nations. When Beltrami told them that he did not belong to any of these nations, they were astonished. He played upon their credulity by telling them that he came from the moon. "Their astonishment was then converted into veneration," wrote Beltrami, "for they adore this planet as a beneficent deity, whose rays enable them to hunt, fish, and travel during the night."

It was among these Indians that Beltrami got his first convincing proof of "the resistless, and . . . fatal allurement of spirituous liquors to the savages." He was eager to obtain a medicine bag, made of the skin of an otter or a beaver, which is used in the medicine dance. But his efforts would have proved in vain had he not bribed with whiskey both the person who gave him the bag and the tribal high priest.

After trying to induce an old chief to give him his bow and quiver, Beltrami philosophized, "Red people give nothing for nothing, any more than white ones." He had offered only flattery, suggesting to the old Indian "that I would immortalize his name, by shewing them to everybody in my own country (the moon), . . . but finding that this sort of Paradise had but little attraction for him, I offered him in exchange some tobacco and gunpowder. Upon this he immediately grew generous, and gave them to me."

It was the custom of the Indians each year to set fire to the brushwood along the river. And so Beltrami beheld a sight both terrible and beautiful. Not only the brushwood, but "the venerable trees of these eternal forests were on fire." From a great distance, Beltrami saw "all the combined images of the infernal regions in full perfection. . . . I have no doubt the devil himself was jealous of it." Reminded vividly of the volcanoes of his native land, the Italian wrote, "The flames towering above the tops of the hills and mountains, where the wind raged with most violence, gave them the appearance of volcanoes, at the moment of their most terrific eruptions; and the fire winding in its descent through places covered with grass, exhibited an exact resemblance of the undulating lava of Vesuvius or Aetna." [9]

Beltrami's impetuous nature and quick temper were demonstrated one day when he came onto the hurricane deck where Major Taliaferro and the ship's fireman, a man named Jones, were engaged in a friendly shooting match, western frontier fashion, at twenty-five cents a shot. While Jones was adjusting the target for Taliaferro's turn to shoot, Beltrami picked up the gun and idly struck the breech on the deck. The gun went off and the ball seared the right side of Beltrami's face. Blaming the fireman for leaving the gun loaded, the Italian went into a rage. He would have struck Jones with the weapon had not the major interposed his arm. The fireman, for his part, was incensed at Beltrami.

"If you had hit me with that gun," he said, "I would have given you the worst beating you ever had in all your born days."

The tension eased for Beltrami's temper quickly cooled and he apologized to Jones for his violent, rash anger. The latter grudgingly accepted the apology. "Stranger, it's all well," he said, "but if you had of hit me with that gun you would have wished you never had." [10]

Aboard the *Virginia* was a family from Kentucky who sought a new life in the Northwest. With them were their arms and baggage, their cats and dogs, hens and turkeys. Beltrami marveled at "the facility, the indifference with which the Americans undertake distant and difficult emigrations." [11]

On May 10, nineteen days after leaving St. Louis, the *Virginia* arrived at Fort St. Anthony after a difficult voyage of 729 miles.[12] It had, Beltrami perceived, "marked a memorable epoch in this Indian territory, as well as in the history of navigation generally." And to the Indians, who viewed with awe the "monster vomiting fire," the steamboat was an object of reverence and fear, and "all the persons on board were in their eyes something more than human." [13]

CHAPTER SEVEN

Fort on the Frontier

SITUATED ON A BLUFF OVERLOOKing the confluence of the St. Peter and the Mississippi rivers, Fort St. Anthony had its beginnings in a treaty which Lieutenant Zebulon M. Pike signed with the Sioux Indians in 1805, whereby nine square miles of territory were ceded to the United States. The consideration was trifling—$200 worth of trinkets and 60 gallons of whiskey—but in 1838 the United States government settled all Sioux claims by paying the Indians $4,000.[1] Fort St. Anthony (later renamed Fort Snelling in honor of its builder, Colonel Josiah Snelling)[2] was in 1823 a frontier fort in the wilderness. It was, in fact, the most distant military post in the Indian territory of the Northwest.

It was not until 1819 that the first United States troops arrived. Commanded by Lieutenant Colonel Henry Leavenworth, the troops camped at the base of the bluff. The following year, Colonel Josiah Snelling succeeded Leavenworth, and it was he who chose the site of the permanent fort on top of the bluff and began its construction. The men of the garrison, paid a bonus of fifteen cents a day in addition to their regular pay of six dollars a month, quarried the limestone, cut the logs, and erected the frontier bastion. The fort was named St. Anthony, after the falls of that name, about eight miles away.[3]

When Beltrami arrived at Fort St. Anthony—he sometimes called it Fort St. Peter, with a fine disregard for accuracy—some construction work was still underway. The Italian immediately noted Colonel Snelling's "activity and vigilance" and praised his wisdom in assigning land around the fort to the soldiers for cultivation, thus keeping them "out of idleness, which is dangerous to all classes of men, but particularly to this." He also commended Snelling for introducing cattle, noting that there were oxen, cows, and horses, but no sheep, probably because of the severe winters.[4]

Major Taliaferro's warm introduction of Beltrami gained a cordial response from Colonel Snelling, who insisted, according to the Italian, that he lodge in his home. Forty years later, Major Taliaferro recalled sharing his own quarters with the Italian traveler, who took his meals at Colonel Snelling's table. However, there is no reason to doubt Beltrami's version: "I could not excuse myself from lodging at the Colonel's, the Commandant of the fort." [5]

Imbued with suspicion of "that hideous police which impedes and molests every movement all over the continent of Europe," Beltrami at first suspected that behind Colonel Snelling's polite gesture was the desire to keep him under strict surveillance. However, he quickly recognized that the colonel's real intention was to pay him respect.[6]

Colonel Snelling and his gracious wife quickly put their guest at ease. Abigail Snelling was the daughter of Colonel Thomas Hunt, and like her husband was born in Massachusetts. Since childhood she had lived in the West

Fort Snelling—The painting by Seth Eastman made about 1851, shows the fort at the confluence of the Mississippi (right) and the Minnesota Rivers, very much as it existed when Beltrami visited there. (From a painting in the Capitol, Washington, D. C.)

and in St. Louis had attended the local French school. Beltrami enjoyed conversing with her in French. When she remarked that her French teacher at Fort St. Anthony had received his discharge, Beltrami volunteered to replace him.[7] Fort St. Anthony, according to contemporary descriptions, although "situated . . . at an immense distance from civilization, [had]many of the comforts of life. The quarters are well built, and comfortable: those of the commanding officers are even elegant." [8] Many of the ladies "would have shone in any circle." The society of the fort at that period was select and aristocratic.[9] Abigail Snelling was a superb horsewoman and was as at home in the saddle as in her own drawing room. Beltrami rode with her and others to the Falls of St. Anthony, only eight miles from the fort, for picnicking and shooting game. He marveled at the waterfall which Father Louis Hennepin, a Belgian friar, had named in honor of St. Anthony of Padua in 1680.

During the two months that Beltrami remained at Fort St. Anthony he spent considerable time among the Indians in the vicinity, exploring the nearby territory, hunting, and collecting Indian artifacts. One day, he brought a Sioux chief into Mrs. Snelling's presence. Pointing to a necklace of highly polished bear-claws around the Indian's neck, he said, "I cannot tempt this chief to part with his necklace, pray see what you can do with him, he will not refuse you."

"He wears it as a trophy of his prowess and a badge of honor," replied Mrs. Snelling. "However, I will try."

After she had used her most persuasive language, the chief responded, "On one condition I will consent; if you will cut off your hair, braid it, and let it take the place of mine, you may have the necklace."

Beltrami joined heartily in Mrs. Snelling's laughter at

The famous Falls of St. Anthony in the Mississippi River, (now in Minneapolis), which Beltrami described in "A Pilgrimage to America."

the Sioux's cleverness in putting an end to the Italian's importunities.[10]

On one of his hunting expeditions, Beltrami's rashness nearly proved fatal. He and a companion were out on the prairie, four days' ride from the fort, when they came upon a herd of grazing buffaloes. Despite the warning of his fellow hunter not to disturb them, Beltrami gave spur to his horse and, waving a handkerchief about his head, galloped into the herd. As the buffaloes retreated, Beltrami rode his horse to the side of a bull and delivered a violent kick into the animal's side as he plunged his hunting knife into the beast's back. Then, even more recklessly, he jumped from his horse and attempted to dispatch the buffalo with knife thrust after knife thrust. The bleeding, infuriated beast turned on his tormentor and, charging furiously, knocked Beltrami off his feet. But for a fortuitous, well-directed shot by his companion, which brought down the buffalo, the travels, explorations, and life of Giacomo Beltrami would have come to an end on the prairie. It is perhaps indicative of his excessive pride that Beltrami does not mention this incident in his book, ignoring it as completely as he did his altercation with the *Virginia's* fireman.[11]

During his stay at Fort St. Anthony, Beltrami witnessed a strange peace parley between the Sioux and Chippewa Indians, whose traditional enmity kept them in a virtually continual state of war. The two tribes had come to the fort to pay their respects to Major Taliaferro, whom they called "Father," and to smoke the calumet of peace. But during the parley, warfare almost broke out between the two tribes. Only the intervention of Snelling and Taliaferro, who were at first reluctant to take any part in the quarrel, prevented open hostilities. They warned both tribes to disperse. To Beltrami's disgust, the In-

Colonel Josiah Snelling, veteran of Tippecanoe and the War of 1812, for eight years commanded at the fort which bears his name. (Courtesy Minnesota Historical Society)

Abigail Hunt Snelling, his attractive and accomplished wife, with her husband, welcomed Beltrami to Fort Snelling and rendered him many kindnesses and much assistance. (Courtesy Minnesota Historical Society)

dians complied. "Everything conspired against my poor notes," he complained, adding:

> I had already perched myself on an eminence for the purpose of enriching them with an Indian battle, and behold I have nothing to write . . . Eskibugekogé [the Chippewa chief] shook hands in all the requisite forms, both with the Sioux chiefs and with all who had a mind. They smoked again perfectly *en régle,*—repeated with great good-will and alacrity the libations of whiskey, and all walked away the best friends in the world . . .
>
> This tragic-comedy, however, procured me what I stand so much in need of,—a hearty laugh; and it was at the expense of the traders. These worthy men trembled for at least four days afterwords, at the recollection of the danger they had run—of losing the advances they had made to the Indians. They thought it scandalously dishonest in them to kill one another before they had killed the beasts whose skins were to constitute the payment.[12]

Encouraged by Taliaferro, Beltrami planned to travel with the major up to the St. Peter River, which had never yet been fully explored. On June 23, Colonel Snelling endorsed the Italian's passport as follows: "By virtue of the authority in me vested, I have authorized the Signor Giacomo Costantino Beltrami, to travel in the Indian Country within the territorial limits of the United States." Taliaferro, in feeble health at the time, begged off from the adventure. Beltrami's pique was reflected in his notes: "It was my intention to proceed thence towards the sources of the Mississippi, which are still absolutely unknown; but Mr. Tagliawar [sic] now feels his health weak, and can proceed no farther. I cannot help fancying that it is intended to lull my projects into lethargy. I am not, however, so easily hushed into inaction and forgetfulness. My constancy against difficulties perpetually in-

Major Stephen H. Long—Beltrami, having joined the expedition headed by Major Long, soon found this officer ungracious and uncooperative and himself being considered as an interloper. Accordingly, he left Long's party and struck out for himself in the wilderness. (Courtesy Minnesota Historical Society)

creases. . . . I . . . shall sustain . . . many a shock and conflict before I surrender." [13]

Despite this bravado, Beltrami had virtually given up the idea of traveling farther north alone and he planned to travel with a Canadian interpreter and an Indian guide, from Fort St. Anthony to Fort Council Bluff on the Missouri and to descend that river to St. Louis and follow his original itinerary down the Mississippi to New Orleans.

But then, without prior notice to Colonel Snelling, there arrived at Fort St. Anthony on July 2, an expedition headed by Major Stephen Harriman Long, a United States topographical engineer, on a mission to locate the source of the St. Peter River. The expedition offered Beltrami an opportunity to push on to the north, and he sought Major Long's permission to join the party "simply in the character of a wanderer who had come thus far to see Indian lands and Indian people."

Vain warnings were given to deter Beltrami concerning the sufferings, dangers, privations of the journey. "As I laughed at these childish terrors," he wrote, "they saw that they had no power over my mind, and that the attempts were wholly vain. . . . They next attacked me on what they thought my weak side,—my purse." His money was, he admitted, in "a declining state" because "the curiosities I had bought of the savages had greatly contributed to diminish its contents." But he had kept some funds in reserve and to add to them he sold his handsome repeater pistol.

When Beltrami finally won Major Long's grudging consent, Snelling and Taliaferro volunteered to advance him some money "with the most honorable and disinterested confidence." Beltrami declined gratefully. Moreover, Taliaferro sent instructions to the Chippewas to see Beltrami safely through their country, if he sought any assistance. The Italian bought a horse from Taliaferro, and secured the necessary provisions for the trip. Before leaving, he distributed trinkets and luxury items in his possession to the Snelling family and to Major Taliaferro for their many kindnesses to him during his stay at the fort.

In the brief time—only a week—that the expedition remained at the fort, Beltrami sensed that his relations with Major Long would be far from cordial. He wrote later, "I foresaw all the disgusts and vexations I should have to experience. . . . but . . . my first intention, that of going in search of the real sources of the Mississippi, was always before my eyes. I was therefore obliged to sacrifice my pride and my feeling of what was due to me . . . and I gave myself up to all I foresaw I should have to endure from littleness and jealousy." [14]

On July 9, the thirty-three-man expedition left Fort St. Anthony. As Major Long recorded in his journal for that date, "Mr. Beltrami, an Italian gentleman . . . an amateur traveler," was a member of the party. The greatest adventure of Giacomo Costantino Beltrami was at last underway.[15]

CHAPTER EIGHT

Two Rivers to Pembina

IT WAS INEVITABLE THAT THE quick-tempered and impetuous Beltrami should clash with Major Long, himself a contentious man throughout his army career and later in civilian life. To begin with, Beltrami considered himself as a paying guest in the party while Long regarded him as an interloper, imposed upon him by Colonel Snelling and Major Taliaferro. Soon their mutual hostility manifested itself openly.

The expedition commanded by Major Long included James Edward Calhoun, an astronomer and nephew of Secretary of War John C. Calhoun; William H. Keating, a geologist and mineralogist, who later produced a narrative of the expedition; Thomas Say, a well-known entomologist and zoologist;[1] and Samuel Seymour, a landscape painter, who helped draw the maps and sketched Indian life. Both Say and Seymour explored the Rockies with Long in 1819. One of the most famous Northwest frontiersmen, Joseph Renville, whose mother was a full-blooded Sioux, was engaged as a guide and interpreter.[2] Other interpreters were Colonel Snelling's nineteen-year-old son, Joe, who also served as a guide.

There was also a military escort, provided by Colonel Snelling, to replace that which had accompanied the expedition from Fort Crawford.

Major Long had orders to explore the St. Peter River (now the Minnesota) to its source and then the Red River of the North to the Forty-ninth Parallel, as far as Pembina on the Canadian frontier. He was also instructed to make a general topographical survey of the country and "to examine and describe its productions, animal, vegetable, and mineral" and to report on the character, customs, and friendliness of Indian tribes in that territory.[3]

The expedition embarked at the mouth of the St. Peter River, which the Dakotas (Sioux Indians) called *Watapan Menesota,* "the river of turbid water," to distinguish it from the Mississippi, whose waters were very clear at the confluence. The Dakotas called the Mississippi *Watapan Tancha,* "the body of rivers," as all other streams were considered branches of this great river. In Algonquian, it was called the *Mechesebe,* from *meche,* "great," and *sebe,* "river."

The expedition divided into two groups, one traveling by land with the horses and mules, the other by river in a boat and four canoes. The two groups were, as far as practicable, to meet each night. The first night they stopped near Oanoska, at the encampment of the chieftain Black Dog.[4] Beltrami had visited this camp and had found it "extremely populous," but a shortage of food had compelled the Indians to hunt for deer and buffalo, and the place was now deserted. An empty hut gave the party shelter from the mosquitoes and the rain, which had been continuous since the departure from the fort. The party passed several other deserted Indian villages at one of which Beltrami noted a dead dog, its head decorated with a plume, hanging in a hut. It was a votive offering to the Indians' "tutelary deities," Beltrami said. He plucked the feather "to enrich my savage collection." Next to women, Beltrami considered dogs the most unhappy creatures among the Indians. Dogs, after having been half-starved and worked hard as hunters and carriers, often ended their lives as a dinner or a sacrificial offering.

One evening, at an Indian camp, Beltrami heard the wailing of a woman in profound anguish. She was tearing her hair as a sacrifice to a relative whose lifeless body was stretched upon a scaffold. Meanwhile, several Indians were eating, drinking, singing, and dancing around another body.

At the Falls of St. Peter, one of the expedition's canoes was swept by the current against a rock. Its sinking included the loss of a keg of tobacco, presents for the Indians, and a considerable store of ammunition, and was a serious blow to the expedition.

On the third day, Beltrami decided to travel on horseback. He observed, "For thirty miles there is a continual series of trees of every kind, and of delicious fruit-bearing shrubs; little smiling meadows; lakes covered with swans and other aquatic birds; delightful plains, and picturesque hills. It seems a fit haunt for nymphs and dryads; unfortunately, however, we found it inhabited by nothing more agreeable than mosquitos and gadflies, which excoriated man and beast. I cannot describe the impression which such a solitude, without a human creature to enjoy its beauty or its riches, makes upon the mind." Symbols carved on a tree by Indians fascinated Beltrami.

A few days later the party experienced a violent storm, which lasted all night. Rain entered the tent on all sides. Beltrami, more thoroughly drenched than any of the others, suspected Major Long had assigned him to the side of the tent most exposed so that he could "reap the glory of struggling valiantly against the fury of the wind, rain, hail, thunder and lightning." The deluge filled the canoes with water, damaging biscuits, coffee, sugar, and other supplies. Because the provisions were diminishing, and because the river had become narrower and more difficult to navigate, Major Long sent some of the men and the canoes back to Fort Snelling. Beltrami complained that although he had contributed more than his share to the common stock, now—only one hundred miles from Fort Snelling—he was beginning to feel hunger.

The party proceeded by land to the Blue Earth River, where the Indians collected the blue earth of its banks to make dye and paint. This river is said to be the highest point reached by the French Canadian fur trader, Pierre Charles Le Sueur, in his travels up the St. Peter River.

A valley of the "most lovely and interesting character" transported Beltrami's imagination to the classical lands of Latium and Magna Grecia. He took advantage of the opportunity to survey this "enchanted ground," going alone so that his reveries could not be broken by "cold-heartedness." Nature seemed to Beltrami to have lavished all her treasures on the beautiful valley watered by the St. Peter River. He was moved to tears. "I should have . . . given myself up to its sweet influence had I not been with people who had no idea of stopping for anything but a broken saddle or some such important incident." The valley "possessed a fertile soil, a salubrious climate, hills and plains adapted to every sort of cultivation, rivers and lakes abounding in fish, shell-fish, and game; delicious groves and forests swarming with deer and with animals of the richest fur, and furnishing every variety of timber for building and cabinet work; and added to all these riches, magnificent stone."

The explorers crossed the Liards, Redwood, and Yellow Medicine rivers, and on July 20 reached Lac Qui Parle. Because rations were short, each member was allowed daily only one biscuit and a thin slice of salt meat.

A party of Sioux Indians, encamped farther north, came to meet them and invited them to a feast. The explorers devoured everything the Indians offered; all tasted delicious, even some roots called "prairie-potatoes," which Beltrami had previously thought detestable.

Major Long, speaking through an interpreter, explained the mission of his expedition. However, when the Indians realized that Long had no gifts for them, they made not the slightest response. As Long described the might of the Great Father (the President), "some yawned, others looked contemptuous," and when Long added that "the expedition was going to trace the remote boundaries of the American territory, all of the Indians showed great annoyance. "Even savages, it seems, are not very fond of seeing other people play the master in their country," observed Beltrami.[5]

On July 22, the expedition reached Big Stone Lake and crossed the St. Peter River, which at this point was a mere ditch. The St. Peter extends about fifteen miles farther to its source, a small lake situated at the base of the Coteau des Prairies. Modern geographers have called this upper part of the St. Peter the Little Minnesota River. However, Major Long did not explore the St. Peter to its ultimate sources. Keating reports in his *Narrative*, "After having left the Big Stone Lake, we crossed a brook which retains the name of the St. Peter, but which cannot be considered as part of that river; the St. Peter may, in fact, be said to commence in Big Stone Lake." [6]

The party arrived at Lake Traverse the next day, where it was made welcome at a post belonging to the Columbia Fur Company. This company had been organized by several Scotsmen who had left the British Northwest and Hudson Bay companies and had acquired a trading license from the Indian superintendent of the territory. Renville, the scout of the expedition, was one of the partners of the Columbia Fur Company. Its location, in the midst of Sioux territory, was ideally situated for fur trading.

Keating in his youthful enthusiasm predicted a successful future for the Columbia Fur Company. Beltrami, on the other hand, suspected that this company could not compete with the South West Fur Company (another American company, owned by John Jacob Astor) and in the long run would have to capitulate to it. His observation came true three years later.[7]

The Great Chief Wanotan of the Sioux greeted the expedition upon its arrival at Lake Traverse and invited the visitors to a feast. Dog and buffalo were on the menu. Beltrami accepted the buffalo meat, which he found very delicious. At the end of the feast, Major Long preached his usual sermon, but again had no gifts to offer. According to Beltrami, Long once more failed to impress the Indians. Chief Wanotan did not even deign to look at the major but amused himself laughing with the "hereditary prince" at his side. Keating reported that the following day the chief came to pay a formal visit. "He was dressed in full habit of an Indian chief; we have never seen a more dignified looking person, or a more becoming dress. . . . We have never seen a nobler face, or a more impressive character than that of the Dacota chief." [8]

Beltrami described Lake Traverse as located on one of the highest points of land that he had seen while traveling with the expedition. Here he was able to observe the humble origins of two great rivers—the St. Peter at Big Stone Lake, the waters of which reach, through the Mississippi, to the Gulf of Mexico; and three miles further up, the Red River, originating at Lake Traverse and flowing north to the Hudson Bay.

During the three days the expedition remained with the Columbia Fur Company, its members assuaged their hunger. Beltrami, horrified at the filth of the huts where the fur traders and their Indian wives were dwelling, asked the major's permission to lodge in one of the expedition tents. But Long, "who wishes to train me to the virtue of patience, refused to have it pitched; and fleas and other vermin concurred with him in pushing the trial to the verge of martyrdom."

The explorers departed from Lake Traverse on July 26. On the same day, buffaloes began to appear on the prairies. Beltrami gave chase and shot one. Two others were killed also, one by a driver and the other by a guide. For the first time the expedition had an abundance of meat. There was no firewood but buffalo dung made adequate fuel. The following day the expedition again met the chief and Beltrami asked Major Long to persuade him to give an exhibition of hunting buffaloes with bows and arrows. Long said he could not stop to do so; however Renville asked the chief, who readily complied and shot a female buffalo. Describing the hunt, Beltrami declared admiringly, "Never did I see attitudes so graceful as those of the Chief." When Beltrami himself shot a buffalo, the chief complimented him, calling him "an excellent shot." [9]

At this point, after guiding the expedition safely through Sioux territory, Renville left the party to return to his personal business affairs. His knowledge of the Sioux language and of Indian customs and mentality and his high personal prestige among the Sioux had assured the expedition of a safe-conduct through their territory. Renville's wise counseling was greatly missed soon thereafter.

The afternoon following his departure, the explorers saw a herd of buffaloes grazing at a distance. Jefferies, a guide who had joined the expedition at Lake Traverse, and Beltrami went after them and shot one. Returning to

This painting by George Catlin gives an idea of the danger to which Beltrami exposed himself when he recklessly rode into a herd of buffalo. (Courtesy Collection of Fine Arts—Smithsonian Institution.)

camp that night, guided only by the campfires, they found the members of the expedition in great agitation. They had met a band of Sioux who appeared hostile, but with Renville gone no one in the party was able to ascertain the Indians' intentions.[10] The Indians, about thirty or forty strong, had intercepted the expedition and insisted that the explorers go to the Indians' camp and visit their old chief. The party declined the invitation because a long journey still lay ahead. The Indians pointed to the sun and said it would be better for the expedition to encamp with them that night. Major Long declined. Joe Snelling overheard the Indians talking about the expedition's horses and inquiring as to which were the best. Major Long mounted his horse and gave orders to march. After the column had proceeded for about a quarter of a mile, several Indians ran to the head of the line, firing across the path of the expedition. One Indian advanced to the head of the column, stopped the horse of the leader, and cocked his gun. The soldier immediately imitated his action. At this moment Major Long came to the head of the column and as the Indians withdrew, he led the party forward. It was night before the party reached the place where they intended to camp. They kindled a large fire to make the camp visible to Jefferies and Beltrami. During the night, six sentinels were posted around the camp and at midnight the expedition resumed its march, or as Beltrami put it, "its flight." [11]

On August 5, at 9 A.M., the expedition arrived at Pembina. It had been a long journey—599 miles, completed in 27 days at an average rate of 22 miles a day.

"This colony, or its skeleton, has been the scene of every species of fraud, crime, and atrocities," Beltrami wrote of Pembina. "It is one of those hideous monsters which avarice and selfishness give birth to wherever they direct their steps." For many years Pembina had been the battleground between the Hudson Bay and the Northwest Fur companies. Lord Selkirk had established the colony of Pembina under a grant of the Hudson's Bay Company, but the governor and the provincial government had favored the North West Company. The two enterprises finally realized that the only beneficiaries of their strife were the American fur companies, and they merged into a single company.

On August 8, at noon, Major Long took possession of Pembina, and the boundary between the United States and Canada was formally laid down at that point. An American Flag was raised, a salute fired, and in the presence of the inhabitants of Pembina, Major Long proclaimed, "by virtue of the authority vested in me by the President of the United States," that the country situated upon Red River, above that point, was within the territory of the United States. Long's action was the most significant achievement of the expedition and one of its main purposes.[12]

For Beltrami, it was the parting with Major Long. He did not wish to continue the trip with one for whom he had no respect and with whom it was evident he was not welcome. The separation was not a cordial one. Major Long noted in his diary: "Mr. Beltrami, our Italian companion, having taken offense at the party, generally, and being highly provoked at my objecting to his turning an Indian out of our lodge, left the party in a very hasty and angry manner." [13]

Joe Snelling and Jefferies left the party, once their services were no longer required, and returned to Fort Snelling. Three soldiers were also released and accompanied Snelling to his father's garrison.[14] Beltrami parted with Dr. Thomas Say with regret, for he had become very much attached to him and considered Say the only true scientist attached to the expedition.

Before striking out on his own for the sources of the Mississippi, Beltrami sought geographical bearings. He asked Long where Pembina was in relation to the North Pole, but the uncooperative major refused to give him the information. Beltrami erroneously decided that Pembina was on the fiftieth degree of latitude when in reality it is on the forty-ninth degree.

When Beltrami told young Snelling of his intended exploration, the latter tried to dissuade him from penetrating into the territory of unfriendly Indians and uncharted regions and rivers. Colonel Snelling had charged his son to protect Beltrami from his own rashness. Snelling entreated Beltrami: "What will my father say?"

Major Long sold the horses and used canoes for the rest of the trip. Beltrami, faced with the same situation, also sold his horse.

On August 9, Beltrami headed into the wilderness, regretfully substituting a small mule for his fine steed. He wrote:

> . . . left behind me Pembenar, [sic] the Major, and my horse. I sold the last, as useless and burthensome in an excursion through unknown regions, thick forests, lakes, and deep rivers. With no slight regret I quitted this faithful friend, Buffalo, the fearless companion of so many chaces and dangers: I should have been not a little glad to have kept him and taken him back with me to Italy. He would have been a living memorial to me of interesting events, and would have excited the jealousy of my Bucharest, whom, if he be still in existence. I should thus have punished for having broken my thigh: could I have enclosed him in my portfolio, he would unquestionably have returned with me. . . .[15]

Thus equipped, the intrepid Bergamasco embarked on his great adventure.

Some of the Indian artifacts which Beltrami brought back to Italy and are now on exhibit in the "Museo di Scienze Naturali" in Bergamo: (1) A War pipe (Sioux), (2) A Scalp of a Sioux, given to Beltrami by the Great Eagle Chief of the Chippewa, (3) A Necklace made of the claws of the White Eagle, (4) A Pipe-bowl (Saukis), (5) A Knife-sheath (Sioux).

CHAPTER NINE

Red Umbrella in the Wilderness

ALTHOUGH NO GUIDE COULD BE found who knew the territory into which Beltrami intended to venture, he was fortunate in inducing two Chippewas, heading for the Red Lake region, to travel with him. A Canadian half-breed, called a *Bois brulé* (burnt wood, so called because of their dark complexion) offered his services as an interpreter. His cart and dog team carried the baggage and the scant supplies.[1]

The Chippewas were seeking help from their relatives to avenge the death of a companion who had been killed and quartered by the Sioux. With a compass to confirm his course, Beltrami resigned himself to follow the Chippewas' chosen trail. For one new to the wild northwest country the journey was an extremely difficult one. But what Beltrami lacked in experience for so quixotic an expedition was more than balanced by his inflexible determination to reach his goal. Besides, to the adventure he brought an abundance of physical and moral courage.

After three days on the trail, the dogs were exhausted and the baggage transferred to Beltrami's mule. As he noted, he continued his journey in the "style of St. Francis." The Chippewas, in a great hurry to reach their destination, pushed on steadily. The *Bois brulé* advised Beltrami not to question their judgment, for they might abandon the expedition without warning. So the Italian pushed on too, resting only when the Indians felt it convenient to stop. He let them smoke his tobacco and eat of his provisions and of the game that he shot. Impressed by the accuracy of his shooting, the two Indians called Beltrami *Kitcy Okiman*, the "great warrior."

Beltrami was pleased with this nickname, which, indeed was a mark of esteem and respect. He hoped that it reflected an acceptance of his leadership, yet he was not sure of this. The experience added to his already considerable knowledge of the Indian and his ways. As long as an Indian remained his own master, he carried his independence proudly, noted Beltrami. But, he said, as the Indian became civilized he changed for the worse. "The Red men . . . most in contact with the whites, are uniformly the worst. The Red women are completely corrupted by their intercourse with the white men. They have all the vices of both races; nor can they find a single virtue to imitate in men who come among them only to sate their sensuality and their avarice." Later, Beltrami observed that "the most subtle and refined malice has now succeeded to that species of simplicity which formerly distinguished them; and they have become more cruel and ferocious in proportion as they have discovered that white men regard them as an inferior *caste* to themselves, appropriate their lands under pretence of defending them, and, while affecting to confer favours by engaging in commerce with them, degrade them into mere slaves of their own avarice."

On August 14, Beltrami and his party arrived at the Thief River. The Indians found their canoe, which they had hidden among the shrubs. They intended to follow the river until it reached the Red Lake River. From Beltrami's description it appears that the Indians were following the East Plains Trail to this point. This trail, after crossing the Red Lake River, continued south, passing some forty miles east of La Biche Lake (later renamed Lake Itasca), and ended at Crow Wing River and finally at the Mississippi.

His interpreter informed Beltrami that at the confluence of the Thief River and the Red Lake River other *Bois brulés* would be found. They had built huts for shelter during their winter hunting. However, they found the place abandoned. When the interpreter, who had volunteered his services only to this point, left, he took with him the cart, the dogs, and the mule. Beltrami, left with the two Chippewas, could communicate with them only by signs. At their next stop the Indians offered a sacrifice to their *manitou*—a stake painted red. The ceremony included Beltrami's tobacco and provisions, but he could stand only helplessly by during the sacrifice of his supplies.

For five or six miles the little party encountered many rapids in the river. To protect the canoe, they were compelled to walk in the water much of the time. While Beltrami was resting during a pause in the journey, he was awakened by a discharge of firearms on the opposite side of the river. A band of Sioux, on seeing Beltrami fled, apparently believing him to be a member of a large expedition. The firing had wounded one of the Chippewas, the bullet passing through the man's left arm, but with no damage to the bone. Boiled roots were applied to the wound and Beltrami's handkerchief served as a bandage. From then on, the two Chippewas imagined Sioux behind every tree and bush, and Beltrami had cause to fear that they were preparing to desert him. To reach Red

Lake by traveling on the river would require about six days; by land Red Lake was only two or three days journey away. Beltrami, fearful of treachery by the Chippewas, kept his musket and sword by his side as he slept. Each night, he fastened the canoe to a tree by one rope and to his leg by another so that the Indians could not take off in the canoe without awakening him.

The party continued in the canoe until they reached a point of the river where the route by land to the lake was much shorter. Here the Indians told him by signs that they were going by the land route and asked him to join them. To do so would have made it necessary to abandon the canoe and most of his provisions and would have placed him at the mercy of the two Chippewas. Because Beltrami believed that by following the river he would reach the lake, he declined their invitation. His suggestion that their *manitou* would take revenge on them for abandoning him did not impress the Indians. Realizing that he could not dissuade them from leaving, he played a grand scene and "commanded [them] by words and signs peremptorily to be gone."

Beltrami now found himself completely alone in the midst of an extensive territory. The closest Indian settlement, at Red Lake, was five days away by river. He had the canoe, his musket and sword, ammunition, and provisions; but he could not travel alone by land without getting lost and he did not know the difficult art of handling an Indian canoe. Beltrami may have realized his critical and perilous predicament but with his usual optimism he tried to make light of it. A good breakfast, which strengthened his body and mind, was his first step in this new life; then he carefully put his gun in order. Beltrami described the first incidents of his new "career":

> I must, said I to myself, leave this place some way or

> other; and I jumped into my canoe and began rowing. But I was totally unacquainted with the almost magical art by which a single person guides a canoe, and particularly a canoe formed of bark, the lightness of which is overpowered by the current, and the conduct of which requires extreme dexterity. Frequently, instead of proceeding up the river, I descended; a circumstance which by no means shortened my voyage. Renewed efforts made me lose my equilibrium, the canoe upset, and admitted a considerable quantity of water. My whole cargo was wetted. I leaped into the water, drew the canoe on land, and laid it to drain with the keel upwards. I then loaded it again, taking care to place the wetted part of my effects uppermost to be dried by the sun. I then resumed my route.

Beltrami spent the first day of his solitude, August 15, dragging the canoe after him with a tow line on his shoulder and an oar in his hand for support. His back stooped, his head bowed, Beltrami held, he said, "conversation with the fishes beneath." By evening he and everything in the canoe were as completely soaked as they had been the previous night. He could not light a fire because the Chippewas had taken with them his steel [flint]. The following noon a storm broke upon him and continued until night, and he and his supplies were again thoroughly soaked. But the next day, August 17, beautiful sunshine greeted the intrepid Italian. Taking advantage of it, Beltrami laid out his food, clothing, gun, and the rest of the baggage to dry. And he himself stretched out in the sunshine.

Beltrami realized that he had to learn to handle the canoe skillfully and he began the ordeal. He succeeded in paddling some small distances where the river was deep, but he became extremely fatigued. So, when the river permitted, he dragged the canoe. When the weather threat-

Beltrami's Red Umbrella which served as "a passport to Safety" among the Indians is still preserved in Bergamo.

ened again Beltrami opened his red silk umbrella and placed it upright in the canoe to cover his effects. The spectacle of his umbrella protecting his baggage while he was forced to travel as "a galley slave," could not fail to amuse the Italian. It was indeed an odd picture: an Indian canoe, dragged by a white man armed with a rifle and walking in the river. Atop the canoe was a great red umbrella.

At about noon on August 18, two Indian canoes approached Beltrami. The Indians halted on the opposite side of the river to contemplate the unusual scene. "What astonished them most was my superbly conveyed baggage," he wrote. "They could form no idea of what *that great red skin* (my umbrella) could possibly be, nor of what was placed beneath it . . ." Beltrami called to them with a friendly: "*Aniscicin nigy* (Good day, my friend)," to which they replied, but such was their surprise, they approached him with great caution.

Beltrami made them understand his plight and asked for someone to accompany him as far as Red Lake. After he had distributed a few gifts, an old Indian consented to guide the canoe to the lake. This assistance saved Beltrami from a very precarious situation; the river was becoming narrower and deeper and it would have soon been impossible for him to proceed much farther.

As the canoe approached the lake, Beltrami felt a strange regret at having left something significant behind him. "You have experienced complete solitude," he told himself. "You have tasted genuine independance [*sic*], you will from this time never enjoy them more. The independance and solitude represented in books, or to be found among civilized nations are vain and chimerical." At that moment he "fully comprehended why the Indians consider themselves happier than cultivated nations, and far superior to them."

The old Indian was a strong rower and they advanced toward the lake rapidly. At night, Beltrami again tied a rope from the canoe to his foot. When a pull on his foot awakened him, he discovered a wolf raiding the provisions in his canoe. A good shot brought it down, but the Indian, fearing that the Sioux were attacking, ran to hide in the forest. He remained there until morning, when Beltrami fired two rapid shots—a sign of friendship among Indians—and thus summoned him back. The old Indian was greatly dismayed, for the wolf was his *manitou*. He expressed his sorrow to the dead animal, insisting that he was not the person who had caused its death.

The following evening, August 19, the old Indian told Beltrami that he had to return to his party. A distant sound awakened Beltrami that night and he saw three or four torches approaching. The visitors were Indian squaws from a nearby encampment who had come to fetch his effects and take him to their huts. The old Indian, eager to return to his family, had summoned them before he left. Beltrami was escorted to a crowded hut occupied by fourteen Indians, nineteen dogs, and a wolf. The wolf welcomed him by tearing his pants, the only serviceable pair he had left. Beltrami lay down to rest in a corner of this "intolerable filthy stable." He was at the end of his physical strength; his body and feet were covered with cuts and bruises caused by the sharp pebbles and shells of the river, the branches of trees, thorns of bushes, and the bites of mosquitoes and other insects. Among the Indians, Beltrami recognized the two who had deserted him a few days earlier.

The next morning, Beltrami asked to be taken to the hut of a *Bois brulé* who lived nearby and for whom he had a letter from Pembina. But the Indians did not wish to leave the camp, because, Beltrami recorded, they were preparing themselves for "yelling, eating, drinking, and dancing" in honor of the Indian killed by the Sioux. Eventually, the gift of a handkerchief induced an Indian to deliver the letter to the *Bois brulé*, who joined Beltrami shortly. The Indian chief, Great Hare, apologized to Beltrami for the two members of his tribe who had abandoned him. The reason, the chief said, was not bad faith, but a desire to bring quickly the news that one of their tribe had been killed. He told Beltrami that no food had been offered him because he had better food than they had; knowing of his generosity, they had helped themselves to his provisions. Finally the Indians asked Beltrami for some tobacco to smoke the calumet of peace. Once the calumet was smoked, Beltrami hurriedly left their camp, fearing the tribe would devour his remaining provisions.

He departed with the *Bois brulé*, who lived about twelve miles from the encampment. They arrived at the hut on the morning of August 21. The *Bois brulé*, son of a Canadian fur trader and a Chippewa woman, lived in miserable conditions. His wife, an infant at her breast and five naked children, appeared to be suffering from malnutrition. They subsisted on fish and green corn. The *Bois brulés*, Beltrami wrote, "are neither civilized nor savage, possessing the resources of neither state, but every inconvenience and defect of both."

At Pembina, Beltrami had been warned about this *Bois brulé*, who had left the settlement after involvement in a crime or serious altercation. But he needed the man's assistance to push on and he had to make the best of the situation. As a precaution against any foul play by the *Bois brulé*, he had "recourse . . . to two expedients . . . to baffle the mischievous machinations of grasping and greedy minds . . . generosity and menace." First the Italian shared his little stock of provisions and linen with the man and his family. Then, "in a firm and elevated tone," Beltrami warned the man that whenever it was necessary, he could "show [his] teeth and exert . . . power."

Beltrami then made it clear that everyone in Pembina knew that he had confided himself to the *Bois brulé's* guidance and both the commandant at Fort St. Anthony (Beltrami called it Fort St. Peter) and the United States government would hold the man responsible for his safety in passing through the Indian territories.

Whatever reluctance the man had shown before—Beltrami recorded that the *Bois brulé* had raised "immense difficulties and invincible objections"—disappeared and the man agreed to accompany him, declaring: "You are a man of ten thousand."

CHAPTER TEN

The Great Discovery

WHEN BELTRAMI FIRST CONCEIVED the idea of trying to locate the source of the Mississippi River—it was when he was still at Fort St. Anthony—he had no way of knowing exactly how he would go about it.

However, after attaching himself to Major Stephen Long's expedition, having learned that its destination was the Canadian border, the intrepid Italian determined to proceed from there southward to reach the watershed from which some of the streams flowed north and some south. There, he was certain, he would find the ultimate source of the Mississippi.

At the time of Beltrami's adventure no one was known to have sought the Mississippi's sources from the north. The expeditions of Zebulon Pike, Lewis Cass and Henry Schoolcraft, which antedated Beltrami's quest, had all approached the area of the source from the South.

Although he was eager to reach the watershed, Beltrami returned to the Indian encampment of Great Hare to engage an Indian to accompany him and his guide and to purchase the canoe to which, with characteristic sentimentality, he had become attached. "I was desirous of having it conveyed, if possible, to my rural cottage, and preserve it with my other Indian curiosities as a memorial trophy of my labours in these my transatlantic *promenades,*" he wrote.

Beltrami and his two companions pushed on, paddling along the western and southern shoreline of Red Lake which he noted was divided into two parts—today, these are known as Upper and Lower Red Lake. Beltrami believed that Red Lake River, by means of which he had entered Red Lake, did not have the lake as its source. This belief became a conviction later, when he reached a stream that flowed into Red Lake from the south. It became clear to Beltrami that Red Lake River entered Red Lake from the south, left by the northwest. "This is the opinion of the Indians themselves," he noted, "and it is not difficult to find arguments in support of it." Later explorations substantiated Beltrami's conclusion.[1]

They proceeded now across lakes, now up streams, now on portages between lakes and rivers. To these, Beltrami often gave names. One day they came upon eight small connecting lakes, set in a landscape that was to the Italian "delightful and enchanting." So captivated was Beltrami with these lakes, whose waters were cold and pure, that he named them for eight members of a family to which he was much attached. This was purely a sentimental diversion for the names survive only in Beltrami's book.[2]

On August 27, after traveling for almost a week, the little party reached the Great Portage River which led to what Beltrami called "a noble lake." It was formed, he observed, like the others, by the waters of the river and had no other issue than the stream's entrance and discharge. Beltrami wrote of this lake:

> Its form is that of a half-moon, and it has a beautiful

> island in the center of it. Its circumference is about twenty miles. The Indians call it *Puposky-Wiza-Kanyaguen*, or the *End of the Shaking Lands*; an etymology very correct, as nearly all the region we have traversed . . . may be almost considered to float upon the waters. The foot sinks in with the turf it treads on, and the latter resumes its level when the foot removes. This lake is situated at a very small distance from high lands, which divide the waters flowing northward from those which take a southerly direction.

One may imagine Beltrami's excitement when he realized that he was close to the watershed, on the southern slopes of which he hoped to locate the source of the Mississippi.

Beltrami made camp there and spent much of the day in shooting wild ducks, some of which were dried and smoked, to add to their provisions. The following morning, August 28, they paddled up the river which entered the lake on its southern side. After traveling about six miles, they came upon the river's sources. These, wrote Beltrami, "spring out of the ground in the middle of a small prairie, and the little basin into which they bubble up is surrounded by rushes. We approached the spot within fifty paces in our canoe." [3]

A short portage led Beltrami to a small hill—the only eminence of any kind he had seen on his journey—and it was crowned by level ground in the midst of which, to Beltrami's surprise, was a small lake, heart shaped and about three miles in circumference. The Italian was on the threshold of his great discovery. Let Beltrami describe what he saw from the hill and its lake: "This lake has no issue; and my eyes . . . cannot discover, in the whole extent of the clearest and widest horizon, any land which rises above the level of it. All places around it are, on the contrary, considerably lower."

He made a thorough study of the area and found no traces that would suggest volcanic action, "yet its waters boil up in the middle." In vain did he try to determine the depth. ". . . all my sounding lines have been insufficient to ascertain their depth; which may be considered as indicating that they spring from the bottom of some gulf, the cavities of which extend far into the bowels of the earth; and their limpid character is almost a proof that they become purified by filtrating through long subterraneous sinuosities. . ."

The sources of the river he had followed, the Great Portage River, were at the foot of the hill and flowed north. Beltrami was certain that the Great Portage and Red Lake rivers were one and the same, and later explorations would lead to the same conclusion. "On the other side, towards the south, and equally at the foot of the hill, other sources form a beautiful little basin of about eighty feet in circumference. These waters likewise filtrate from the lake, towards its southwestern extremity; and THESE SOURCES ARE THE ACTUAL SOURCES OF THE MISSISSIPPI! This lake, therefore, supplies the most southern sources of Red . . . and the most northern sources of the Mississippi—sources till now unknown of both."

Beltrami, in his moment of ecstatic joy, named the lake Lake Julia in honor of his late dear friend, Countess Giulia Spada de Medici and the sources of the two rivers, the Julian sources of Red Lake River (Beltrami had decided to call it Bloody River) and the Julian sources of the Mississippi.

One does not have to imagine what went on in Beltrami's mind when he discovered what he was certain was the source of the great Father of Waters. He tells us, in his most extravagant prose: "Oh! what were the thoughts which passed through my mind at this most happy and

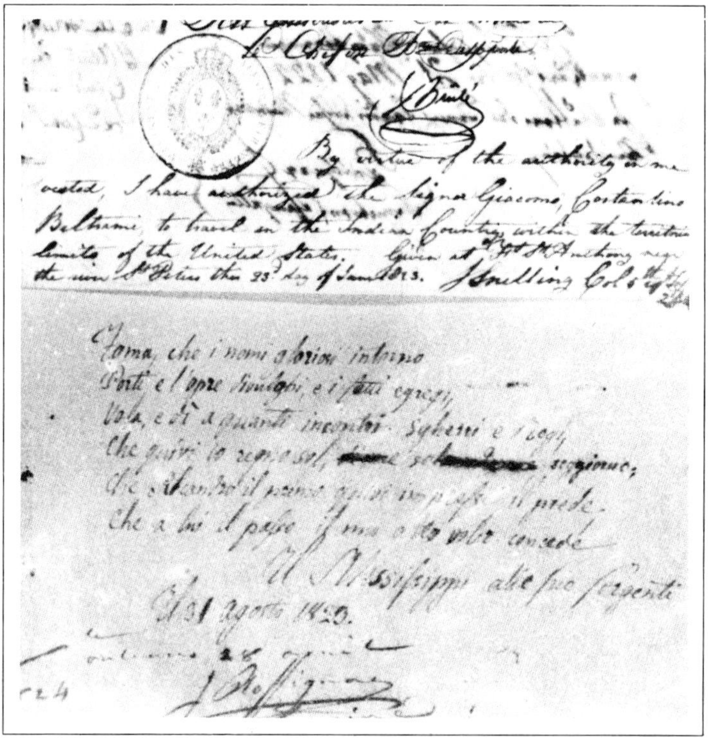

By virtue of the authority in me vested, I have authorized the Signor Giacomo Costantino Beltrami, to travel in the Indian Country within the territorial limits of the United States. Given at Ft St Anthony near the river St Peters this 23d day of June 1823. J Snelling Col 5th Infy

Fama, che i nomi gloriosi intorno
Porti e l'opre sublimi, e i fatti egregi,

Il Mississippi alle sue sorgenti
li 31 agosto 1823.

The endorsements on Beltrami's Papal States' passport tell the story of his start from Fort Snelling, his completion of his Mississippi adventures at New Orleans and the moment when he recorded, in verse, what he considered to be his discovery of the source of the Mississippi.

brilliant moment of my life! The shades of Marco Polo, of Columbus, of Americus Vespucius, of the Cabots, of Verazani [sic], of the Zenos and various others, appeared present, and joyfully assisting at this high and solemn ceremony, and congratulating themselves on one of their countrymen having, by new and successful researches, brought back to the recollection of the world the inestimable services which they had themselves conferred on it by their own peculiar discoveries, by their talents, achievements, and virtues."

Had Beltrami possessed scientific instruments, he would have been able to support his claim of discovery with the precise latitude and longtitude of Lake Julia. But as he said, if he had had such instruments, he could not have satisfactorily availed himself of them. "Astronomy," he regretted, "was but slightly touched on in my education." [4]

Beltrami was so enraptured by his discovery that it took three calls by his companions to get him to dinner. But not before he had scrawled on his passport a six line poem in Italian commemorating the day, August 31, 1823, and the place.[5]

Beltrami hoped that he could travel the Mississippi from its source to its mouth and thus become "the only individual[s] who ever traversed the whole of its course, as we were the first to discover its sources." But he put aside the idea, because the narrow strait of about three miles from the small basin, south of the hill, to Turtle Lake was obstructed by almost impassable brambles and brushwood. "If I had not been afraid of adventuring my canoe . . ." he wrote, "I should have commenced the navigation from the very spot on which they spring."

In imagination, Beltrami confessed, he had conceived the mighty Mississippi as springing from precipitous mountains "down which the waters of this monarch of rivers rushed in mighty waves," and was astonished to find the great river's origin in "one eternal flat of swampy ground." He elaborated on the Mississippi's modest beginnings: "The majestic river, which embraces a world in its immense course, and speaks in thunder in its cataracts, is at these its sources nothing but a timid Naiad, stealing cautiously through the rushes and briars which obstruct its progress. The famous Mississippi, whose course is said to be twelve hundred leagues, and which bears navies on its bosom, and steamboats superior in size to frigates, is at its source merely a petty stream of crystalline water, concealing itself among reeds and wild rice, which seem to insult over its humble birth."

Beltrami thought he was the first white man to explore the labyrinthine Turtle Lake, which had no other outlets than the entrance and issue of the Mississippi. He was in error when he declared that "neither traveller, nor missionary, nor geographer, nor expedition maker ever visited this lake." Unknown to him, of course, and indeed to the world for more than half a century was David Thompson's *Narrative,* covering his travels in Minnesota, 1784–1812. Thompson, a Canadian fur trader and geographer, had traveled the area Beltrami covered in 1798 and he had recorded his opinion that Turtle Lake "is the source of the famous Mississippi River in the most direct line." Thompson's *Narrative* was not published until 1888—sixty-five years after Beltrami's book was published.[6]

When Beltrami saw that the stream issuing from Turtle Lake was safe for navigation, the party got underway on September 2. His Indian guide, who had hunted in the area, said that nearby was Heron River which they could explore and return to Turtle Lake by a short cut. The Indian induced Beltrami to make the excursion by suggesting that bears could be hunted on the way. They returned to Turtle Lake the next evening.

A source of wonderment to Beltrami was the skill with which beavers built their dams—"a manner which would not disgrace a corps of engineers," he said. He was amazed at the "order and discipline" that existed in beaver colonies. "Beavers are divided into tribes and sometimes in small bands, each of which has its chief," wrote the Italian. ". . . each tribe has its peculiar territory." Continuing, he added:

> If any foreigner be taken in the act of marauding, he is delivered over to the chief, who, on the first offence, chastises him with a view to correction; but, for the second, deprives him of his tail, which is considered as the greatest disgrace to which a beaver can be exposed: for the tail is the carriage on which he conveys stones, mortar, provisions, &c. and it is also the trowel (the figure of which it represents exactly) which he uses in building. This violation of international rights, however, is considered among them as so great an outrage, that the whole tribe of the mutilated culprit take up arms in his cause, and proceed immediately to obtain vengeance.
>
> In this conflict, the victors, availing themselves of the customary rights of war, expel the conquered from their home, take possession of it themselves, appoint a provisional garrison for the occupation, and eventually establish in it a colony of young beavers. In this connection, another circumstance relating to these truly wonderful creatures will appear not less astonishing.

Beltrami related that the Indians told him some of them had been eye-witnesses to a duel between the chiefs of two rival tribes of beavers who terminated the "quarrel by a single combat, in the presence of the opposing armies, instances of which have occurred in various nations; or by a conflict of three with three, like the Horatii and Curatii of antiquity." While reporting this, Beltrami may have had his doubts; nevertheless, he wrote: ". . . it is so extraordinary, that I leave you to credit it or not, as you may think proper."

Beltrami noted that the Mississippi, from where the Heron entered it, flowed constantly through the marsh land, for its banks were submerged though sometimes varied by prairies and forests. He found "its bed . . . always very deep, and its course gentle and uniform." After forming four lakes, which Beltrami called the lakes of Providence, the meandering Mississippi entered Red Cedar Lake to the south and flowed out to the east. It was here, on September 4, that Beltrami camped.

Of Lake Traverse (now Bemidji Lake), Beltrami wrote: "This lake communicates westward by a passage two or three miles long with another lake that the Indians call *Moscosaguaiguen*, or Lake de la Biche, which receives no tributary stream, and seems to draw its waters from the bosom of the earth. It is here in my opinion, that we shall fix the western sources of the Mississippi." He estimated the distance of Lake La Biche from the Red Cedar Lake to be forty or fifty miles.[7]

Three days later, Beltrami and his company were at Leech Lake where he discovered numerous encampments of Chippewas. The tribal feud had divided the group into two factions—one under Pokeskononepe, Cloudy Weather, the other under Esquibusicoge, Wide Mouth. Beltrami arrived when agitation was at its highest. The son-in-law of Cloudy Weather had been killed by a Sioux a few days before; at the same time the tribe received the news of the Indian killed on the Red Lake River. Wide Mouth was preaching immediate war, and a council of the elders had been called. On his arrival, Beltrami was asked to attend. Some of the Indians remembered having seen him at the gathering of Indians at Fort St. Anthony.

The Indians told Beltrami that the Great Spirit had sent him to advise them as he was a friend of their

"Father," Major Taliaferro. Cloudy Weather, although greatly aggrieved by the killing of his son-in-law, believed that he should not sacrifice his tribesmen in a war for personal vengeance. He sought the advice of "that man of another world, who had smoked with them the calumet of friendship." Beltrami replied that he was a stranger to America and the only advice that he could give was that they consult their Father, Major Taliaferro, who loved them. The Indians accepted his suggestion and Cloudy Weather prepared to accompany him to Fort St. Anthony to consult Taliaferro.

The day and night of September 12 were, Beltrami confessed, the most terrible of his life. "I tremble whenever I think of them," he wrote. English agents had given some of the Indians several barrels of whiskey. Virtually, the entire tribe, noted Beltrami, "soon became violently heated and maddened by it."

Although up to then, the Italian had noted that Indian women "preserve to themselves the strictest sobriety," he was startled on this occasion to observe that "the women were more completely inebriated than the men." Beltrami gave a graphic description of the orgy that resulted:

> . . . all were plunged in the most frightful state of intoxication.
>
> The hell of Virgil, and of Dante, or even that painted by Orcagna, at St Maria Novella in Florence, in a style so deeply impressive, are only faint sketches in comparison with that full display of terror and death presented in the tragedy now acted; a tragedy exhibiting in all their horrors the Bacchantes, the Furies, the Eumenides, Medusa, and all the monsters of history or fiction.
>
> Hatred, jealousy, long standing quarrels, mortal antipathies, all the ferocious passions, were in most exasperated excitement and conflict. The shrieks of the women and children, mingled with the yells of these cannibals,

Beltrami repeatedly deplored the practice of the fur companies in debauching the Indians with strong drink. This portrait of a drunken Indian was done by Seth Eastman. (Courtesy Kennedy Galleries, Inc.)

and the bayings of dogs, added the tortures of hearing to all the agonies which appalled the sight.

Beltrami positioned himself on a small mound, his cutlass in his belt, his gun in hand, and his sword, half unsheathed, at his side. "I remained a spectator of this awful scene, watchful and motionless," he said. "I was often menaced, but never answered except by an expressive silence, which most unequivocally declared that I was ready to rush on the first who should dare to become my assailant."

But when, during the orgy, he saw that his host, Chief Cloudy Weather, was being attacked by two savages with knives, he rushed into the melee, with his *Bois-brulé* and the Chief's daughter at his side. "We saved him by disarming of their knives the two assassins who had attacked him, and against whom, merely with a small piece of wood, he defended himself like a lion."

The following day revealed the toll of the brawl: two Indians dead, twenty-four wounded, seven mortally. Among the dead was the Indian who had accompanied Beltrami from Red Lake. The *Bois brulé*, who had been cut on the hand, wished to return to his family, and Beltrami bought him a canoe and paid him for his service.[8]

Beltrami attributed "the progressive extinction of the Indians," in part, to "the ravages of whiskey," which despite government regulations in 1817 and in 1822, was freely supplied by the agents of the great fur companies. John Jacob Astor's American Fur Company, although ostensibly obeying the law, violated it consistently. Not only did Astor's firm continue to supply whiskey to the savages, but it became the largest supplier of them all.[9]

Beltrami and Cloudy Weather immediately left for Fort St. Anthony. A storm forced them to camp at the opposite bay. Next morning, they stopped at a post of the

North West Company, where Beltrami endeavored to hire another *Bois brulé* as an interpreter. None could be found so Beltrami and Cloudy Weather continued their trip down the river, unable to communicate with each other. When they arrived at Sandy Lake, they found another establishment of the Southwest Company with a Canadian in charge. Here Beltrami purchased wild rice, potatoes, and a kettle for cooking his food, and the party remained four days. He engaged another Indian to help with the boat, and now had two companions with whom he could not communicate. Beltrami was eager to push on for winter was approaching and they experienced the first frost.

The Mississippi now flowed through territory contested by the Chippewas and Sioux, an area where the two tribes carried on a perennial war. Recalling the impression on the Indians his red umbrella had made, Beltrami again raised it over his canoe. The red umbrella announced to the warring Indians the passage of a stranger, "a foreign and neutral power," as Beltrami put it. No Sioux interfered with the progress of Beltrami's canoe down the river.[10]

Impatient with the slow progress in navigating the river, Beltrami repeatedly tried to tell the two Indians to speed up. But his impatience did not effect the imperturbable Indians. Finally, Cloudy Weather gently tapped Beltrami with his pipe as if to warn him to keep quiet, as though he was saying: "Be patient. I will see you safely to my Father's place." Beltrami understood and controlled his restlessness as they pushed on. A small band of Indians from Sandy Lake, en route to Fort St. Anthony to see Major Taliaferro, overtook them. When one morning they heard the roar of water over rocks, Beltrami realized they were approaching the Falls of St. Anthony. It was a joyful sound to the Italian, announcing his return to civilization after nearly three months of life in the wilds.

Beltrami prepared himself for a formal arrival at Fort St. Anthony. He shaved with a rusty razor, with neither soap nor mirror; he bathed in the river, and dressed himself in a suit of skins sewn together in the Canadian fashion. He wore a hat formed by two pieces of bark. The Indians announced their coming by firing their guns, and with songs, cries, and beating of drums. Colonel Snelling, Major Taliaferro and all the officers of the fort came down to the river to meet the canoes. When they recognized Beltrami, whom they believed lost, they expressed "lively joy" at finding him safe.

"I saw in the expression of their physiognomies," wrote Beltrami, "both a movement of surprise, and sentiments of affection and friendship. The excellent Mr Tagliawar [sic] embraced me in the most cordial manner, and the colonel, his respectable wife, and his children, received me with demonstrations of the most lively joy. I was much moved, and could not help shedding tears of gratitude and attachment. . . . They were indignant against Major Long for acting towards me in the miserable manner that he did."

Later, at the fort, Beltrami spoke with some Sioux Indians, who had followed the progress of the Chippewas' canoes on the river. They told him that the red umbrella raised over his canoe had discouraged them from attacking the party.

Out of concern for the *Bois brulé* guide of Red Lake Beltrami asked Major Taliaferro to assist the man and his destitute family. Taliaferro, who knew the *Bois brulé* as being unfriendly to the Americans and cooperating with the British, nevertheless, at Beltrami's urging, arranged a job for him.[11]

On September 25, Beltrami bade farewell to his friends,

Colonel Snelling, Major Taliaferro, and the colonel's wife and children.

Beltrami travelled down the Mississippi River to St. Louis on a keel-boat. "I could, indeed, never restrain my admiration of it," he declared. "What a beautiful—what a majestic River! . . . I found excellent company in some gentlemen travelling from the military academy at West Point, near New York . . . These gentlemen are going with the rank of officers to Fort Council Bluff. They are well informed, as those generally are who come from that establishment, which is the Polytechnic School of the United States." On October 20, Beltrami reached St. Louis. His experience had been a magnificent and unbelievable one—a journey in the wilderness for nearly three months. Three weeks later, Beltrami, accompanied by his Indian collection and canoe, left St. Louis for New Orleans.[12]

CHAPTER ELEVEN

Une Ville Charmante

DOWN THE MISSISSIPPI, THE STEAMboat *Dolphin* made its tortuous way for more than a month before it reached the levee at New Orleans. Beltrami, who was now short of funds, was among eight deck passengers who made the journey from St. Louis. The *Dolphin's* cargo included more than 500 packs and bales of peltries.[1]

Beltrami had with him his collection of Indian articles and also his canoe, which was attached outside the rail. The voyage was hardly underway when the steamboat went aground below St. Louis. To Beltrami's keen disappointment the canoe was irreparably damaged. His sentimental attachment to the canoe was considerable, for as he said, doubtless with exaggeration, it had conveyed him "in safety amidst a thousand rocks over a space of more than two thousand miles." Captain Honey, indifferent to the loss of the canoe, ignored the protests of his sentimental passenger. Beltrami characterized him as being "wholly destitute of politeness." To console himself, he composed a Latin epitaph for his canoe which he called his "Dilecta Liburnica," pleasant little boat.

The immensity of the Mississippi River never ceased to amaze Beltrami. The merging of its tributaries with the great river was, he said, a spectacle of a "most delightful and impressive character." He was fascinated by the encounter of a stream, struggling to maintain an identity before mingling its waters with the Mississippi in a majestic sweep. He called the Mississippi River the first river in the world, and wrote: "I declare and will maintain it to be so, without fear of contradiction." He continued,

> Judge now whether another such river can be found on the globe which thus communicates with every sea and at various points, which combines so many wonders with such great utility, which surveys more than one hundred steam-boats gliding over its waters, with an infinite number of other vessels freighted with the productions and manufacture of both worlds, and to which futurity promises such brilliant destinies. Judge whether the Mississippi be not the first river in the world!
>
> The Amazon, and the la Plata, may exceed the Mississippi in the volume of their waters; but in all other respects, far more important, they cannot be compared with it; and what confers on the latter a decided superiority is, that along the whole extent of its banks man can breath[e] the air of liberty, and industry meets with no restriction.

Another astonishing characteristic of the Mississippi, Beltrami found, was the constant shifting of the stream so that often landmarks, houses, and even towns found themselves on opposite banks from their original relation to the river's course. One such case he stated was at the confluence of the Ohio and Mississippi rivers, where a house, which he had noticed at the river's edge six months earlier, was now high and dry, about fifty feet from the bank.[2]

The *Dolphin* made frequent stops on its way to New Orleans and Beltrami kept notes on the towns along the way. Memphis was "an inconsiderable village"; and Natchez was "the first place after St. Louis which presents traces of an advanced civilization." Moreover, he thought Natchez to be "really beautiful" and its environs contained "a great number of handsome country-seats, where the planters for many years made and enjoyed ample fortunes." Beltrami noted the ravages of yellow fever which Natchez had experienced that summer: "Nearly four hundred persons have died, and the emaciated and pallid faces that met my eye in every street, plainly indicated that numbers of the living had narrowly escaped." Baton Rouge he found to be "a pleasant little town, situated on a small eminence, . . . the last to be found on the Mississippi." The seventy-five mile distance between Donaldsonville, a village also on Bayou LaFourche, and New Orleans, he wrote, "may be considered as one continued town, consisting of the habitations of planters." [3]

The *Dolphin* reached New Orleans late in the afternoon of Friday, December 13. The port teemed with activities, with river steamboats, ocean vessels, schooners, fishing boats and flatboats crowded against the levee.[4]

New Orleans' "astonishing prosperity," impressed Beltrami. This, he explained was due to its being placed under the government of a nation whose rulers, instead of being the people's tyrants, are merely the depositaries of their will—it is only owing to its freedom from all vexatious restrictions on its industry, commerce, and prosperity, from capricious abuses of power, profligate monopolies, and selfish corporations." He considered New Orleans, "more brilliant than any other American city that I have seen." He hailed its 45,000 inhabitants as "a prodigious population for a place which may be said to have just emerged from a swamp, and where the yellow fever and the natural insalubrity of the climate every year effect deplorable ravages." As Beltrami entered New Orleans after dark, he imagined himself in a grand capital, for the streets were well lighted with reflecting lamps and were crowded with carriages. The city in 1823 had already begun to pave its streets.[5]

Five daily newspapers were published in the city, three of these in both French and English. New Orleans, compared to the capitals of Europe for amusements, he concluded. Horse races, dramatic presentations, concerts, balls, and "gaming academies of every description." Six gambling houses were licensed by the legislature in 1823 to operate in New Orleans and its suburbs on payment each of a state tax of $5,000. Beltrami expressed amazement that there were more gambling houses in New Orleans than in Paris. "I did not expect to find this passion in such intense operation among a commercial, active, and republican people," he acknowledged. "I supposed it confined to courts, dissipation, and idleness."

Beltrami had letters of introduction to several important people in New Orleans and a letter of credit from the banking house of Baring & Co. of London. The latter restored Beltrami's now almost depleted funds, for he had arrived in New Orleans eight months later than originally planned. He quickly felt himself at home in New Orleans, because he could converse freely in French with nearly everyone.

An inveterate playgoer, Beltrami attended performances at the St. Philip Street Theater and the Orleans Theater in the old French quarter and the new American Theater on Camp Street, in the American quarter above Canal Street. He praised the performances, especially because they were free from "those dirty buffooneries and obscene equivoques which, among nations pretending to greater refinement, frequently put decency and modesty to the blush." The French Theater had accessory rooms and offices unequaled, Beltrami suspected, by "any provincial theater in Europe; particularly a large room, where subscription, dress, and masked balls are given; . . . where the beautiful Creoles fascinate and dazzle under the forms of the Graces, and where luxury and decorum are in happy combination. Louisiana is indebted for this elegant establishment to Mr. [John] Davis, who sacrificed to it a great part of his fortune. . . . The French theatre, to the precision and fascination of the machinery introduced upon the stage, adds decorations of the most superb description and almost marvellous effect. M. [J. B.] Fogliardi, who is the painter, has obtained a well-merited reputation." [7] Fogliardi, a resident of New Orleans between 1821 and 1825, was the decorator and painter of the Orleans Theater and had opened what is believed to be the first drawing academy in New Orleans in 1823 at St. Ann and Rampart streets. James H. Caldwell, owner of the American Theatre in the Faubourg St. Marie on Camp Street between Gravier and Poydras, introduced gas illumination in New Orleans in his theater. The "gas machine," imported from England, created a sensation among the patrons. Later two gas lamps were added to the front of the theater and more lights were extended to Canal Street to give patrons the benefits of a sure friendly illumination coming from the Vieux Carre.

From December 13, 1823, to April 28, 1824—the period of Beltrami's visit in New Orleans—The St. Philip Theater, the Orleans Theater, and the American Theater produced no less than forty operatic works, concerts, and ballets—an impressive number of events for only a part of the musical season. Concerts were frequently given for special benefits, and were followed by balls, which always assured a good attendance.[8]

One could not reside in New Orleans at this time without feeling the presence of Père Antoine (Antonio de Sedella, a Spanish Franciscan friar), who for fifty years (1779–1829) exerted a profound influence on the religious life of the City. Of Père Antoine Beltrami wrote, "I cannot, and indeed ought not, to quit New Orleans without mentioning . . . Father Anthony. He is a venerable Spanish Capuchin, who for eight and forty years had devoted his life to imparting the consolations of faith to this population, with simplicity, and without either fanaticism or intolerance. . . . and he is, by the inhabitants in general, highly esteemed and beloved." [7]

Beltrami visited Chalmette, where the Battle of New Orleans was fought just nine years before he reached the city. He praised the Americans, "nearly all militia . . . collected in haste," who defeated the British on January 8, 1815. He lauded General Andrew Jackson's "courage, skill, and firmness," which were matched by his troops. "The ladies of New Orleans on this occasion distinguished themselves by their humanity as much as their brothers and husbands did by their valour," Beltrami added. What impressed him most in this military campaign was the personality of General Jackson—a general who had convincingly routed some of the best seasoned troops of that era, a general who had been carried in triumph through the public streets of New Orleans, yet who voluntarily at the same time submitted to the civil tribunals of his country and paid a fine of $1,000.00 imposed on him by a federal judge for a violation committed in connection with his military duty.[8]

New Orleans social life was so full that Beltrami could not find the serenity required to put together the notes on his travels. Seeking a secluded spot in the countryside not far from the city, he moved to a plantation in St. James Parish, above New Orleans. Preparing a narrative of his wanderings and observations was no easy matter for his notes were recorded on scraps of paper and even on the bark of trees.

Meanwhile, on November 27, 1823, *L'Ami des Lois* published on its editorial page a description of the expedition of Major Long. The same journal announced on December 2, that the expedition had arrived in Philadelphia. Neither report mentioned Beltrami's name, which angered the Italian.

He feared that someone might claim for himself his discoveries. On January 29, 1824, Beltrami issued a public notice in both *Le Courrier de la Louisiane* and *L'Ami des Lois*. The notice, which was repeated several times, stated:

> G. C. Beltrami has the pleasure to announce to the government of the United States and its citizens, that in a voyage undertaken last summer . . . he discovered the most northern and western sources of the Mississippi, . . . completely unknown until the present time . . . [He], being the only one who has traveled the Mississippi in its entirety, from its true sources to its mouth . . . the description which he proposes to make public will serve . . . to make known many important points and also to rectify many gross mistakes which appear in the best maps . . . At present he is occupied putting in order the notes and observations made during his long and difficult voyages in unknown territories and among savage nations. Consequently he puts the public on notice, in order to defeat the efforts of those who have followed or may follow his footsteps, trying to arrogate for themselves a glory that does not belong to them, and to take away from him the fruits of his labor, research and expenses.

Working steadily on his manuscript, Beltrami had it ready for the printer in March and on April 12, *La Dé-*

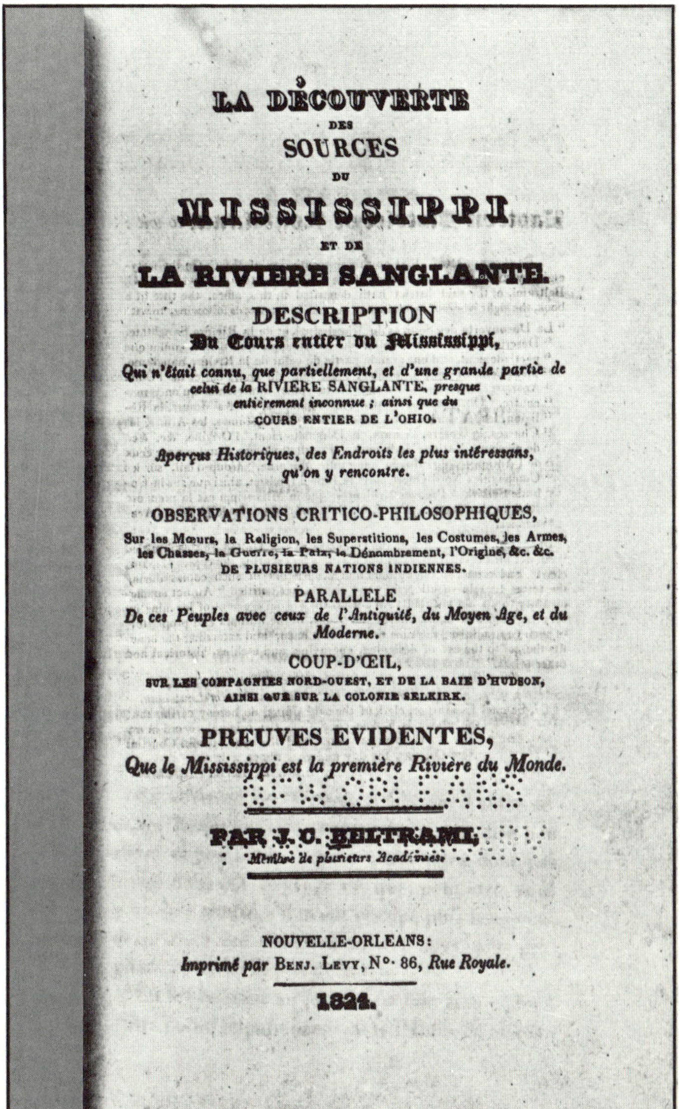

LA DÈCOUVERTE
DES
SOURCES
DU
MISSISSIPPI
ET DE
LA RIVIERE SANGLANTE.

DESCRIPTION
Du Cours entier du Mississippi,
Qui n'était connu, que partiellement, et d'une grande partie de celui de la RIVIERE SANGLANTE, *presque entièrement inconnue ; ainsi que du* COURS ENTIER DE L'OHIO.

Aperçus Historiques, des Endroits les plus intéressans, qu'on y rencontre.

OBSERVATIONS CRITICO-PHILOSOPHIQUES,
Sur les Mœurs, la Religion, les Superstitions, les Costumes, les Armes, les Chasses, la Guerre, la Paix, le Dénombrement, l'Origine, &c. &c.
DE PLUSIEURS NATIONS INDIENNES.

PARALLELE
De ces Peuples avec ceux de l'Antiquité, du Moyen Age, et du Moderne.

COUP-D'ŒIL,
SUR LES COMPAGNIES NORD-OUEST, ET DE LA BAIE D'HUDSON, AINSI QUE SUR LA COLONIE SELKIRK.

PREUVES EVIDENTES,
Que le Mississippi est la première Rivière du Monde.

PAR J. C. BELTRAMI,
Membre de plusieurs Académies

NOUVELLE-ORLEANS:
Imprimé par BENJ. LEVY, N°. 86, *Rue Royale.*

1824.

Beltrami, on arrival in New Orleans, published through Benj. Levy his "La Découverte des Sources du Mississippi," of which this is the title page.

couverte des Sources du Mississippi et de La Rivière Sanglante came from the press.

Beltrami's announcement in *Le Courrier* and *L'Ami des Lois* stated:

> ". . . my work is not being written for speculation. My purpose is to offer to the public what I believe can be useful and enjoyable to the people of the United States, of general interest to my country and perhaps to the world. . . . I will believe myself repaid for my labors, sufferings, and great expenses . . . if the reading of my work will win the approval and good will of cultured people and be useful to society. The manner in which this work has been received by the members of the legislature of this state . . . gives me hope, that it will not be received less favorably by the other citizens of Louisiana." [9]

The book, which sold for $3.00, was praised by the public, by city and state officials, and generally by the press. In a letter to Beltrami, the secretary of the Louisiana Legislature, Joseph F. Carronge, wrote, "The inhabitants of Louisiana cannot but feel the most profound gratitude, the most special predilection for the learned and courageous man, who with great sacrifices, and painful deprivation has discovered the sources of the river to which they are indebted for the greater part of the prosperity of their country." Governor Thomas Bolling Robertson sent his appreciation and congratulations to the author. Horatio Davis, secretary of the Senate, wrote that the senators of Louisiana had commanded him to express their congratulations and appreciation. Mayor Roffignac of New Orleans declared, "That as your country was the cradle of the great man who discovered this hemisphere, now it is destined to be that of the man who wrested from it secrets, the disclosure of which calls you to the public esteem." [10]

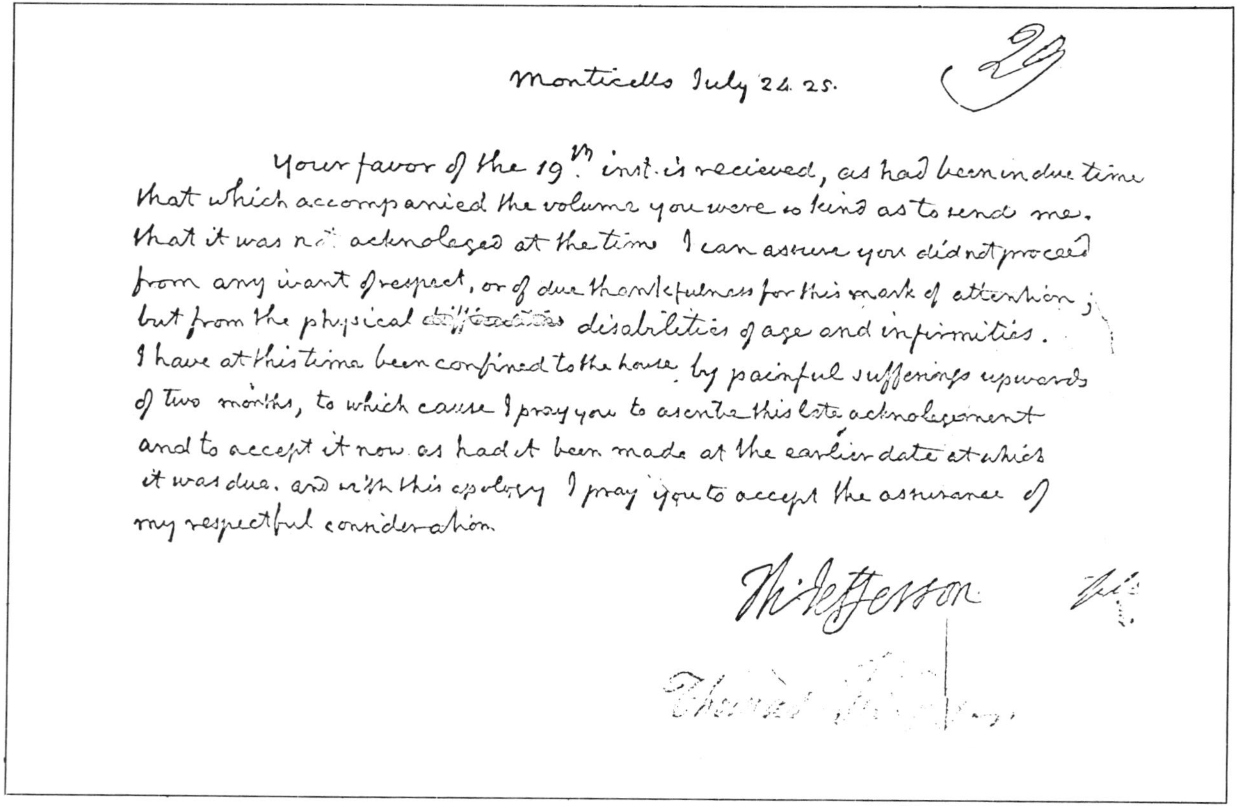

Monticello July 24. 25.

Your favor of the 19th inst. is recieved, as had been in due time that which accompanied the volume you were so kind as to send me. that it was not acknoleged at the time I can assure you did not proceed from any want of respect, or of due thankfulness for this mark of attention; but from the physical disabilities of age and infirmities. I have at this time been confined to the house by painful sufferings upwards of two months, to which cause I pray you to ascribe this late acknolegement and to accept it now as had it been made at the earlier date at which it was due. and with this apology I pray you to accept the assurance of my respectful consideration.

Th: Jefferson

Thomas Jefferson's acknowledgment of Beltrami's gift of his book.

The press was also laudatory. The *Courrier* commented:

> It may truly be said that M. Beltrami's work is the only one giving a full knowledge of the Mississippi, and of the tribes living on its banks. Before he discovered the *real sources* of that great River . . . the White Bear Lake, the Leach Lake, the Red Cedar Lake, were disputing, each other, the honor of being the sources of the finest river in the world; and MM. Pike and Schoolcraft that of having discovered it. When we reflect that a Stranger, assisted by only a few interpreters, has done more, alone, than all the Expeditions undertaken at great expenses by the Government; when we think of the dangers to which he has been exposed; the toil and fatigues he has endured, the obstacles of all kinds which he has had to surmount to achieve such an undertaking, we can not help admiring the perseverance and courage of that distinguished individual, and regretting that the glory of the enterprise do [does] not belong to one of our citizens.

The *Argus,* which had been rather cool at Beltrami's first claim of the discovery, devoted a three-column editorial to praising the exploit and Beltrami's perseverance, courage, and sagacity. The writer regretted that the lack of instruments deprived the friends of science of observations that might have established beyond doubt Beltrami's right to that important discovery.

The *Louisiana Gazette* published a letter in French on the editorial page, praising Beltrami's exploit. "His work breathes the love of humanity and of liberty, his statements are those of a man without prejudices and of great experiences, his morals are pure, his sentiments are of the highest, and finally in his work reigns a character of truth which does not leave any doubts as to the authenticity of the facts which he describes and which will bring to the author the esteem of all that will read it." [11]

However, Beltrami's book was not without its critics. In a letter to the *Argus* signed "Small Gullet," the writer, without mentioning Beltrami by name, poked fun at "a voyage that has been so much talked about!" [12]

Beltrami's lack of scientific observations and measurements at the Lake Julia sources of the Mississippi plagued him for many years. Criticism was often repeated on this point, sometimes in good faith and sometimes maliciously by those who did not wish him well.

His book duly launched, Beltrami prepared to continue his travels to Mexico as originally planned. He left New Orleans, "une ville charmante," with some regrets after his four-month visit. When Beltrami asked Pere Antoine's advice for his trip to Mexico, the old friar told him, "The priests and the monks are the masters of the country." It was important to be in their good graces, Père Antoine said and suggested that Beltrami offer them gifts of European design, which were more appreciated there than money.

On April 28, he sailed from New Orleans on the sloop *Eliza-Ann* for Tampico. The schooner stopped at English Turn, a few miles below New Orleans, to pick up a passenger, who, wrote Beltrami, boarded the schooner there to avoid his creditors in New Orleans. He was a Kentuckian and was full of liquor and in boarding the ship fell into the river and had to be fished out by members of the crew. Perhaps for the first time in his life, Beltrami remarked, the Kentuckian had imbibed more water than whiskey. During the trip to Tampico the man drank as if "he had a hole in his stomach, smoked all day like a chimney, snored all night like a Badger, spit everywhere." Beltrami thought he had never seen a man more animalistic in his intemperance and his absence of all social manners.

Contrary winds delayed the *Eliza-Ann* at the mouth of the river, which Beltrami found "dreary, monotonous, and depressing." Tedious nights were punctured only by the abundant and noisy marine life and by the huge mosquitoes which Beltrami termed "bird-mosquito" It was not until May 14 that Beltrami reached Tampico. For nearly a year he traveled in Mexico, the result ultimately being two engrossing volumes.[13]

After an absence of almost a year, Beltrami returned to New Orleans from Mexico on the schooner *Sally Ann*, on April 27, 1825.[14] A week later, the *Courrier* carried a public announcement by Beltrami:

> . . . I hope that those who have had the patience to read my Decouverte des Sources du Mississippi or some of my other essays, all of them written hurriedly, have not found in me any pretentions to appear a savant; they have found only a man avid to see, to compare and to learn. It was with this sole view that I desired also to make a tour . . . of . . . [Mexico] . . . and have visited the most interesting regions of the vast Mexican empire . . . Minerals, silver, gold and some stones have been collected by me, which do not yet belong in the nomenclature of the mineralogists and geologists . . . In libraries and elsewhere, I have discovered objects which add to the history of the manners and of the Arts of these aborigines . . . Fragments of paintings of ancient artists and rare plumage of birds . . . and a book in agave paper . . . which preserved for us the Papyrus of Anahuac written in the Axtec language . . . This book is perhaps the most precious finding of my research and the most satisfactory compensation of my toils. The persons who wish to take advantage of my short stay in this city and see this small collection, may call at my lodging, Rue Royale, No. 244, above the academy of Mr. Fogliardi . . . the price is one piastre [dollar].[15]

Shortly thereafter Beltrami left New Orleans for Philadelphia and New York. He again sailed on the Mississippi, retracing his old course to the confluence of the Ohio River and from there to Pittsburgh. He never returned to New Orleans.

CHAPTER TWELVE

Beltrami Under Attack

THE RELATIONSHIP BETWEEN THE romantic traveler and the army topographical engineer did not end with Beltrami's departure from Major Stephen H. Long's expedition on August 9, 1823. Beltrami in his book, *La Découverte,* had unnecessarily criticized in detail Major Long's leadership of the expedition. A copy of Beltrami's book reached Long and William H. Keating in Philadelphia, where the latter was assembling the reports of various members of the expedition and writing the *Narrative.* Over a nine-month period, the twenty-four year old Keating received from the government two dollars a day for writing it "in a candle-lighted room in Philadelphia." The government also paid the room rent, provided fuel, candles, paper, ink, and pens. The result was a highly interesting and informative narrative, a remarkable work for such a young man. Dedicated to President James Monroe, the book, although published commercially, was in effect a semiofficial publication of the United States government.[1]

Beltrami's participation in the expedition was mentioned only in a footnote in Keating's narrative:

"An Italian whom we met at Fort St. Anthony attached himself to the expedition and accompanied us to Pembina. He has recently published a book entitled: *La découverte des sources du Mississippi et de la Rivière Sanglante,* which we notice purely on account of the fictions and misrepresentations which it contains." [2] The footnote, carrying the initials "S.H.L." was written by Long. Beltrami did not learn of Long's attack until his arrival in Philadelphia in July, 1825. At once, he wrote to Keating and to the Philadelphia publishers of the *Narrative,* H. C. Carey and I. Lea, for an explanation.

Carey and Lea answered that they did not know that such a note had been included in the book and added, "We can with truth say we regret to have been instrumental in publishing what should have been disagreeable to you as it should to every other gentleman." [3] On the same date, July 15, 1825, Keating wrote to Beltrami that the note appearing on page 314 of the *Narrative* under the initials "S.H.L." "was introduced by Major Stephen H. Long of the United States Army, under whose orders I was then acting." [4]

Incensed over Major Long's deliberately derogatory remark, Beltrami immediately sought a confrontation with him. But Long was away from Philadelphia so Beltrami, on July 19, wrote him with indignation which his studied language could not disguise:

> You may recall that I promised when I left you in Pembina that I would come to Philadelphia to ask you for an explanation for the indignities to which you submitted me during the time I traveled with you in the savage country. Then I respected in you the Chief of an expedition which belonged to the Government and the people which are so profound in my esteem and in my veneration. I have learned that you are absent, but where you have gone I have not been able to learn.

> The insolent note inserted in page 314 of your Second Expedition against this *Italian*, and of which the compiler and the editor accuse you of being the author, makes it indispensable that you give me an explanation in the usual manner of a man of honor.
>
> I am awaiting your reply in New York at the address of Messrs. Le Bay and Bayard.[5]

Major Long made no response to Beltrami's letter but, in later editions of Keating's book, published in London in 1825, and in the United States, the offensive words "fictions and misrepresentations" were deleted and the note was changed to read, "An Italian gentleman, whom we found at Fort St. Anthony, asked, and obtained leave to travel with the expedition: he continued with them until the 7th of August. This is the gentleman who has lately published an account of his discoveries on the Mississippi; we have read it." [6]

Another unpleasant situation developed for Beltrami in Philadelphia. He learned that a shipment of 400 copies of the *La Découverte,* which he had sent to that city from New Orleans immediately on its publication, to be distributed in other eastern cities, had arrived but had not even been unpacked. Beltrami's book became available in the East only many months after Keating's *Narrative* was already in the hands of the public. Thus the attack on Beltrami's credibility in a semiofficial publication reached the reading public before his own book was distributed. It was not, moreover, until 1828 that an English edition of his work was published.

A letter published on July 29, 1825 by the New York *Commercial Advertiser,* expressed indignation over the suppression of Beltrami's book in the East: "It may appear strange that such a work has not been seen sooner before the public in this part of the United States! . . . In the eastern states, the compilers and merchants of the expedition of Major Long, found in it an *unseasonable* witness. They conspired and concealed it. . . . It is but a few days since a determined hand rescued the book from the tomb to which envy and self-interest had consigned it." [7]

Robert Walsh, Jr., co-publisher of the Philadelphia *National Gazette*, who had contributed "valuable notes" to the *Narrative* of Major Long's expedition in his capacity as a secretary of the American Philosophical Society of Philadelphia, had editorially attacked Beltrami and his claim. On Aug. 12, 1824, the *National Gazette* carried the following statement: "An Italian traveller in this country, named Beltrami, claims the merit of having discovered the sources of the Mississippi! Within the last twenty years they have been visited by nearly one hundred persons now residing in St. Louis, Missouri. A map may be seen there, constructed by Messrs. Clarke [*sic*] & Lewis almost twenty years ago, in which the sources of the river are plainly laid down, and as accurately marked as is necessary to understand the geography of the region." [8]

Upon learning of the editorial the proud Bergamasco could no longer contain his anger. After trying in vain for twelve days to see Walsh to demand an explanation, the indignant Beltrami wrote to him on July 28. ". . . if in your article of August 12, 1824 you tried to be wicked, I was not surprised because every one knows you to be a malicious man, and who feels it necessary to be one. I also attribute to ignorance, the lies which you have published with the greatest impudence. It is common knowledge that Lewis and Clark never constructed any maps nor did they ever ascend the Mississippi. Pike and General Cass, the only ones who have gone in search of the sources, did not succeed in their enterprise; but as I see you are an insolent individual and wilfully insolent against my person, who has shown you nothing but courtesies, I am compelled to ask you for an 'explication solennelle.' " Nothing in Beltrami's papers suggests that Walsh ever replied to the challenge.[9]

Whatever the merits of the criticism leveled at Beltrami's book it was prejudged before it had general distribution. This harsh reception was keenly felt by Beltrami, for the slurs of Long and Walsh were repeated by others. For many years, Beltrami felt compelled to defend himself on what he considered unjust attacks on the veracity of his narrative.

Beltrami, himself, had been intemperate in criticising the leadership of Major Long. Long possessed a very stubborn nature and he was unable to accept criticism or opinions different from his own. A taciturn, gloomy, and unimaginative man, he often came into violent conflict with people who disagreed with him. Years later he had a dispute with Jefferson Davis, then Secretary of War, and he was relieved of his duties in 1853. It was inevitable that the personalities of Long and Beltrami should clash in the wilderness and the Italian must share some of the blame for their mutual uncordiality and distrust.

Many years later in his autobiography Major Lawrence Taliaferro recalled, from their very first encounter, Major Long was not well disposed to Beltrami. Long, in his diary entry of July 9, 1823 had recorded: "Mr. Beltrami, and [sic] Italian gentleman of the order of noblen [noblemen] also joined our party as an amateur traveller. He had ascended to Ft. St. Anthony in the steam boat *Virgin*[*ia*] . . . and learning that our expedition was on the march, awaited three weeks for our arrival, with the view of accompanying us." Major Long was careless with the facts, for neither Beltrami nor anyone else at Fort St. Anthony had prior knowledge of Long's expedition until it arrived at the fort on July 3. It had traveled ahead of any possible communication to Colonel Snelling at the fort concerning the expedition and its expected arrival.

Major Long always seems to have thought of Beltrami as an interloper who had forced his way into an official military mission of the United States, a rather suspicious foreign character who was always taking notes. Long could not believe that a man of Beltrami's age would submit to the hardships and dangers of such a trip just to visit new territory and to learn about the Indians.[10]

CHAPTER THIRTEEN

The Embattled Pamphleteer

STILL INDIGNANT OVER CRITICISM of his book, his discovery, his veracity, Beltrami published a 36-page pamphlet in New York in December 1825 defending himself against the attacks.

In *To the Public of New York and of the United States,*[1] Beltrami reacted with particular sensitivity to the Philadelphia critics, especially Robert Walsh:

> At Philadelphia, the editor of the National Gazette, the friend of Major Long, (and whom all the world knows very well,) has prostituted truth, evidence, and the good sense of the public, to the necessity, which he cannot resist, of being malicious and rude. See his paper of the 11th or 12th August, 1824.—Mark, I have committed no other fault towards him, but that of treating him with much politeness; which I have done also towards many others who have conspired with him, and sought, by secret and base devices, to prejudice the public of Philadelphia against my poor book.

Beltrami's pamphlet reviewed the reviews of his book in the New York press. The *Commercial Ad-*

vertiser, he remarked, had "exaggerated praise" for his book. The *Evening Post* praised his work but criticized "his disposition to satire"; the *National Advocate* gave the book what Beltrami calls "equivocal praise"; the *Review* praised and condemned it at the same time. The *New York Review* merely announced the title of the book.[2]

Beltrami did not remain sedentary for long, for he decided to visit Haiti. This trip nearly cost him his life for he contracted yellow fever in February, 1826. His strong constitution and his refusal to allow the doctor to bleed him, led to his recovery within eight days. Beltrami returned to New York with copious notes of his trip and some Haitian literature and newspapers. He intended to write a book, *The Black Republic*, but it was never written and his notes were lost after his death.[3]

In October, 1826, Beltrami left for England. The following March, the *London Magazine* reviewed *La Découverte*. The reviewer praised Beltrami and his exploration: "His style is original and brilliant, and a rich and fertile imagination gives a vast charm to his composition." The long review ended with a wish that Beltrami's work be made known to England. This encouragement moved Beltrami to publish a new edition of his travels in English.

A Pilgrimage in Europe and America, published in London in 1828, included the eleven letters of *La Découverte* addressed to Countess Geronima Compagnoni and the four letters of *Deux Mots sur les Promenades de Paris à Liverpool*. In addition, two letters never published before were included. The two French books were much enlarged and expanded in the English edition and there were several changes of dates in the letters. Arrangements had also been made for a French edition of *A Pilgrimage* to be published in Paris. As soon as the pages of the London edition were off the press, they were quickly translated into French and sent to Paris. Unfortunately, the editor and publisher went into bankruptcy and this project had to be abandoned.[4]

In England *A Pilgrimage* attracted generally favorable reviews. Evidently the English edition was made available to the press late in December, 1827. The London *Weekly Review* of December 29 carried a three-page review, labeling the author a "clever, lively, enterprising traveller" who was a hero to "his sweet self" and to his "still sweeter countess to whom all of his letters are addressed." However, the *Literary Chronicle* termed Beltrami's general style "egotistical, declamatory and commonplace." The *Monthly Review* published a long review, objecting to the epistolary form to communicate important geographical discoveries. Notwithstanding such faults, the reviewer respected the "valuable matter of his work" and considered the two volumes "both curious and important." He concluded that Beltrami's work "should not be forgotten."

The London *Times* emphasized "one most interesting part" of *A Pilgrimage,* the account of the author's travels among various Indian tribes. The reviewer "follows the traveller with the liveliest interest; we see through [Beltrami's] eyes the most striking and picturesque events of savage life." He concluded by recommending the work to readers. The *Scots Times* of Glasgow in a five-column review paid homage to Beltrami as a partriot driven out of his country by an oppressive foreign regime. The author was termed "a well informed, liberal, acute, and generally speaking important traveller." Yet "certain imperfections in his style and mode of writing" were noted. The reviewer concluded that *A Pilgrimage in Europe and America* has "added to our geographical knowledge by an important discovery" and has "illustrated many strange and unknown features of man's physical and moral character in a savage state." The *Atlas*, the *Examiner*, and the French newspaper *Le Furet de Londres* also published favorable reviews.[5]

However, some of the acrimony from Philadelphia found its way to London. A strangely vitriolic attack appeared in the *Quarterly Review*. The article begins with a personal thrust: "This ex-judge of an ex-court in an ex-kingdom would seem by his own account to have been sent into exile, without trial." It continues, "What the nature of his offense was we are left to conjecture. . . . A more exquisite dandy . . . thrown into the desolate regions of North America, could not have been imagined." Although the reviewer promises that he "shall not waste much time or paper upon the gentleman," he continues the attack on Beltrami for eight pages. "It required some little ingenuity to continue to swell out a whole volume of five hundred pages, in ascending the Mississippi to its sources, and from thence dropping down to its mouth," he scoffs. Half of Beltrami's book is taken up with descriptions of "adventures among the Indians, with long and tedious details of their religion, and their medicine-bag—how they dance, and drink, and smoke and fight—what long speeches they make," and with "words, words words."

The critic complains, "[Beltrami's] grand object was to discover the sources of the Mississippi, which had, in fact been clearly discovered . . . by Mr. Schoolcraft two or three years before the date of his pilgrimage! . . . he (Beltrami) must blush to see in what a silly as well as shameful manner he has falsified the geography of this portion of North America." If Beltrami insisted on preaching "any more false facts," the reviewer threatened, he would be "tempted to give him a specimen of rather severe discipline." At the end of the article, the critic mentions Keating's *Narrative* and quotes the derogatory footnote on

Beltrami which appeared in the first edition. A remarkable similarity of style can be detected between this review and the article in the Philadelphia *National Gazette* of August 12, 1824, which Beltrami attributed to Robert Walsh. Walsh had contributed articles to British publications and in 1827 adopted the name *Quarterly Review* for his American publication. Is it possible that he was the author of this later attack? [6]

Beltrami immediately answered the *Quarterly Review* with a pamphlet, "Beltrami's 'Pilgrimage' and the Quarterly Review." In justification of this pamphlet, he wrote to the editor of the *Globe*, on April 5, 1828, "I am publicly provoked, in the most provoking manner, by an unprovoked libeller; and I must raise my voice, even before the public." Despite the unfair attack, he felt confident in the justice of English public opinion. Although "this libeller may be an English subject . . . he cannot be an Englishman." [7]

CHAPTER FOURTEEN

The Chateaubriand Enigma

IF THE EGO OF GIACOMO COSTANtino Beltrami needed flattering after the critical assaults upon his book, he received it from one of France's most distinguished literary figures, François Auguste René Chateaubriand.

Chateaubriand paid Beltrami the double compliment of quoting from his *Découverte, etc.*, with and without attribution. In the preface to his *Voyage en Amérique* Chateaubriand quoted almost three pages from Beltrami's book, stating: "He is a foreigner who writes French; it is easy to recognize the taste, the traits, the character and the justifiable pride of the Italian Genius." [1]

But both contemporary critics and later authorities have noted that Chateaubriand "lifted" more than fifty pages of Beltrami's text without so much as hinting that the material was not original with him as the result of his own travels and observations.

In 1828, an unidentified writer in the *Foreign Review and Continental Miscellany*, reviewing Chateaubriand's *Les Natchez, Voyages en Amérique et en Italie* and *Études Historiques*, charged the

French writer with plagiarizing from Beltrami.

"Beltrami writes in a wild and eccentric style," the article stated, "and his political opinions are ridiculous in the extreme, but it is evident, in spite of his folly and his falsifications, that he has been in America. We shall not be so uncivil as to insinuate that M. de Chateaubriand is in the contrary predicament." Continuing, the writer charged:

> . . . but it is beyond question, that he has made the most liberal use of M. Beltrami's work, and passed off the observations of the Italian gentleman, which are dated in 1823, as his own original observations, purporting to be extracted from his private journal of 1790. That he had seen M. Beltrami's *Pilgrimage* cannot be denied, for he quotes it in his prefactory chapter. . . .
>
> . . . If the reader feel any curiosity on the subject, let him compare the accounts of Indian manners in Beltrami . . . with Chateaubriand . . . and he will find the latter almost identical with the former. Or take the account of the beavers from Beltrami, compared with that from . . . Chateaubriand, and the identity will be recognized at once. There are many other passages equally striking; . . . It is impossible that these can be merely accidental coincidences, for, to say nothing of the multitude of passages, even the particular *niaiseries* (frivolous trifles) are followed. In the description of the beavers, for example, Beltrami foolishly compares some combats of these animals to the battle between the Horatii and Curiatii; and the same piece of nonsensical pedantry is repeated in the same manner in M. de Chateaubriand's account of the same contests.[2]

A twentieth century scholar, Ernest Dick, found that of 180 pages of the *Voyage en Amérique,* Chateaubriand borrowed 149 pages from other authors, including François Charlevoix, William Bartram, J. C. Beltrami, J. E.

The Church "Chiesa Prepositura" in Filottrano where Beltrami is buried.

Bonnet, Jonathan Carver, Le Page Du Pratz, Alexander Mackenzie, and others. Dick compared the Chateaubriand and Beltrami books, paragraph by paragraph, and demonstrated that 56 pages of Chateaubriand's *Voyage* were borrowed from Beltrami's *La Découverte.* The appropriation from Beltrami covers a considerable part of the *Voyage,* particularly the sections on animals (castors, bears, deer, buffaloes, reptiles), Indian customs (marriages, children, funerals, dances, hunting, war, calendars, medicine, language, religion), Indian tribes (the Natchez, Hurons, Iroquois, and other Indians of North America), and the itinerary along the Ohio and Mississippi.[3]

Chateaubriand, a superb stylist, in "borrowing" from Beltrami, greatly improved the French of the Italian. Prudently, he openly acknowledged his debt to Beltrami in three places in his book. Aware of Chateaubriand's indebtedness, Beltrami referred to Chateaubriand's reliance on his work in his preface to *Le Mexique*: "In France, *The Revue Encyclopédique, The Revue Britannique, The Journal des Voyages, The Annals de la Societé Géographique,* etc., etc., have also written more than once of the *Découverte* . . . ; and M. de Chateaubriand has cited me with praise and has borrowed some pages for his *Voyage en Amérique.*" [4]

Perhaps out of respect for what Chateaubriand stood in the political arena and because of their friendship, Beltrami did not question the fact that fifty-six other pages were used by Chateaubriand for which no credit was given. The fact that some literary reviews had noted the similarities of the two books must have nourished Beltrami's ego. To have so well-known a figure in the French literary and political world, perhaps the greatest French writer of the Romantic era, borrow a "few" pages from his book was tribute to his talent which Beltrami would not dilute with resentment.

It has been well-established that Chateaubriand could not have made the journey he describes in his *Voyage en Amérique*, in the time he was in this country.[5]

That a writer of Chateaubriand's stature would commit plagiarism so flagrant is an enigma. But no less an enigma was Beltrami's uncomplaining willingness that his writings should win delayed public favor under someone else's name.

CHAPTER FIFTEEN

Minnesota Remembers

IN 1829, WHEN BELTRAMI REACHED Paris, the days of the Bourbon Restoration were numbered. Paris seethed with political unrest and the July Revolution of 1830 was soon to topple the regime of Charles X and bring Louis Philippe to the throne as King of the French. What part, if any, Beltrami played in the fast-changing events is not known, but his friends in France were prominent in political life including Chateaubriand; Jacques Laffitte, defender of a free press and premier of France in 1830–31; General Lafayette, member of Parliament and commander of the National Guard; and Benjamin H. Constant, named president of the Council of State by Louis Philippe.

Beltrami received many honors during the five years he lived in the French capital. Sponsored by Louis J. Jullien, founder of the *Revue Encyclopédique*, Beltrami was elected a member of the Geographical Society of France. Later he was admitted to membership in the Universal Civilization Society, the Geological Society of France, and the Historical Institute of France.[1] Representing the latter two organizations, he attended an international scientific meeting at Stuttgart in 1834 and participated actively in the deliberations of that congress. Officials of the Historical Institute considered the Italian one of the most distinguished members of that scientific association.[2]

Following publication of *Le Mexique* in 1830, Beltrami produced a small book, *L'Italie et l'Europe*, in 1834.[3] In that year he built a small villa in the valley of the Neckar, near Heidelberg and he retired to Germany. In a letter in 1836 from his German retreat to the secretary of the Historical Institute, Monglave, Beltrami, on a note of sadness and acceptance of fate, reviewed his past struggles and accomplishments, the lack of recognition of his discoveries and the appropriation by others of them. "Each man has, without a doubt, a mission on this earth," he declared. "I believe I have accomplished mine." Similar views were expressed in a letter to the president of the Académie des Sciences on July 2, 1837.[4]

Three years after settling in Germany, he wearied of the sixteen years of self-imposed exile and returned to his estate in Filottrano in Italy. His health began to fail but, amid friendly neighbors he spent his last years restoring his neglected properties and helping in the care of the poor and needy.

Beltrami did not live to see the fulfillment of his dream of an independent Italy, for he died on January 6, 1855, at the age of seventy-six, a decade and a half before unification was achieved.

His affection for the poor and the needy and his disdain of ceremony were expressed in his will: "My funeral will be very humble . . . my tomb will be that of the poor, [the common grave] joining them in death, as I have always sympathized and helped them in life." He left funds to be distributed to the poor, to his servants and to the attendants at his funeral. He instructed his heirs that "the

Villa Spada—Home of the Countess Giulia Spada de Medici, Beltrami's dear friend, at Filottrano.

small red Morocco box, at present in the yellow room, be forever kept in the house, to preserve a noble memory, a noble friendship; also the folio therein which illustrates it." Obviously a reference to Giulia Spada de Medici, who willed it to him at her death in 1821. The red box contains a china tea set for two.[5]

Posthumous recognition came to Beltrami in his native Bergamo. His heirs donated all their uncle's documents, correspondence, and manuscripts to the city, and also all of Beltrami's Indian artifacts, and the red silk umbrella which had so profoundly aided his travels.

In 1856, the Athenaeum of Bergamo opened its academic year with an address by Count Pietro Moroni, mayor of the city, on the life and writings of Beltrami. Articles about his travels by the historian Gabriele Rosa were published in the *Gazzetta Veneta* of April 20 and 21, 1856. Three years later, Bergamo held a display of Beltrami manuscripts, documents, Indian souvenirs, and artifacts, including the red umbrella which served him well in the wilderness. An imaginative portrait of Beltrami by Enrico Scuri, painted for this occasion, and donated by the artist, a native of Bergamo, was unveiled.[6]

The *Geographische Mittheilungen* of Gotha, Germany, reported Rosa's articles and in this manner information about Beltrami's death reached America. Colonel Alfred J. Hill,[7] former secretary of the Minnesota Historical Society, who was then on duty in Washington, read the article in the German publication. He wrote to the mayor of Bergamo, seeking information concerning Beltrami. Noting the "valuable discoveries in reference to the sources of the great river Mississippi" that Beltrami had made, he added: "The Minnesota Historical Society . . . has always been desirous of doing justice to the early explorers of the Northwestern Territory . . . but had been unable to obtain any biographical information other than

In her will, the Countess Giulia Spada de Medici left this tea service to Beltrami and in his will he requested that the set be kept forever in the same room in his house. It remains there to this day.

the brief notes in his *Pilgrimage*." In response, Camozzi Vertova, mayor of Bergamo, sent Colonel Hill a pamphlet on Beltrami dedicated to the Minnesota Historical Society. Its thirty-four pages contained biographical data, letters, and a reproduction of Scuri's portrait of Beltrami. Shortly thereafter, the Minnesota Historical Society memorialized the State Legislature to honor the discoverer of the Lake Julia sources of the Mississippi by creating a County of Beltrami, to be "formed out of the region he particularly explored." The document detailed Beltrami's travels and the hardships he encountered in his solitary journey from Pembina to the headwaters of Turtle Lake and the Lake Julia source of the Mississippi and said that after discovering these sources Beltrami followed the Mississippi "to its confluence with the stream from Lake Itasca which it equals in the volume of water discharged: thence he descended by the Mississippi to New Orleans." The Minnesota Legislature responded favorably and in 1866, Beltrami County, much larger than it is today, was created.[8]

Henry H. Sibley, president of the Minnesota Historical Society and the first governor of the state, sent the mayor of Bergamo an official copy of the decree creating Beltrami County. He included a letter from now venerable Major Taliaferro, with his photograph and various publications. Sibley declared that if Beltrami could revisit the land of his former wanderings "he would be the amazed and delighted spectator of the marvelous transformation which has been wrought in less than half a century. His eyes would rest upon cities, towns and villages situated on the very spots where he had accepted the hospitality of the savages in their rude wigwams; and the evidences of a young and vigorous civilization would meet his astonished vision on the broad prairie, which he had known only as the resort of countless herds of the bison and of the elk."

Sibley concluded with a rhetorical question: "Is it strange that we, who live to profit by the toils and exposures of the noble men who first explored and brought into notice, this *terra incognita,* which is destined to become the home of millions of freemen, should seek with earnestness and zeal to redeem their names from oblivion, and to assign to each the honor due him as a pioneer in the great work?"

Thus did Minnesota honor Giacomo Costantino Beltrami who, with his red umbrella and an unswerving determination made history in the wilderness.[9]

CHAPTER SIXTEEN

Many Men, Many Sources

AS ONE REVIEWS BELTRAMI'S AND other claims of discovery of the source of the Mississippi River, these questions inevitably are raised:

What constitutes the true source of a river?

Is it located at the greatest distance from the river's mouth?

Is it in a direct line to its mouth?

Or, has a river many sources?

Various theories as to the source of the Mississippi River have been put forward. In 1798, David Thompson, British geographer and astronomer employed by the North West Company, identified Turtle Lake as "the source of the famous Mississippi River in the most direct line." [1] Zebulon M. Pike, when he reached Leech Lake in 1806, exclaimed: "I will not attempt to describe my feelings on the accomplishment of my voyage, this being the main source of the Mississippi." [2]

In 1820, Henry R. Schoolcraft, a member of Michigan Territory Governor Lewis Cass' expedition, advanced Upper Red Cedar Lake (Cassina Lake) as "the true source of the Mississippi River." [3] But in 1832, the same Schoolcraft, guided by the Indian chief Oza Windib, on reaching Lake La Biche, renamed it Itasca Lake and called it "the source of the Mississippi." Lieutenant James Allen, a member of the same expedition, said that this lake was "the true source and fountain of the longest and largest branch of the Mississippi."

This Lake La Biche which already bore three names—the Chippewas called it Omoskos Sagaigon, the French La Biche, and the English Elk—to which Schoolcraft gave the fourth name of Itasca. The word was manufactured from the six middle letters in the Latin *veritas caput*, (true head), hence source. Years later, Schoolcraft invented a myth about an Indian girl named Itasca whose tears for a lost lover formed the spring which created the lake and the Mississippi as well.[4]

Beltrami had learned from the Chippewas that their forebears had long believed that Lake La Biche was the source of the Mississippi. Although he reached a point within 40 miles of Lake La Biche, he did not push further west to explore it. Relying on the information the Indians had given him, Beltrami had concluded that "Lake de la Biche . . . receives no tributary, and seems to deliver its waters from the bosom of the earth. It is here, in my opinion, that we should fix the western sources of the Mississippi."

And thus, nine years before Schoolcraft, Beltrami recognized Lake La Biche—Schoolcraft's Itasca—as *a* source of the Mississippi, albeit he erred in considering it to be a secondary source, with Lake Julia as the great river's primary source.

Beltrami furthermore followed ". . . the theory of ancient geographers, the sources of a river which are most in a right line with its mouth should be considered its principal sources, and particularly when they issued from a cardinal point and flow to the one directly opposite." [5]

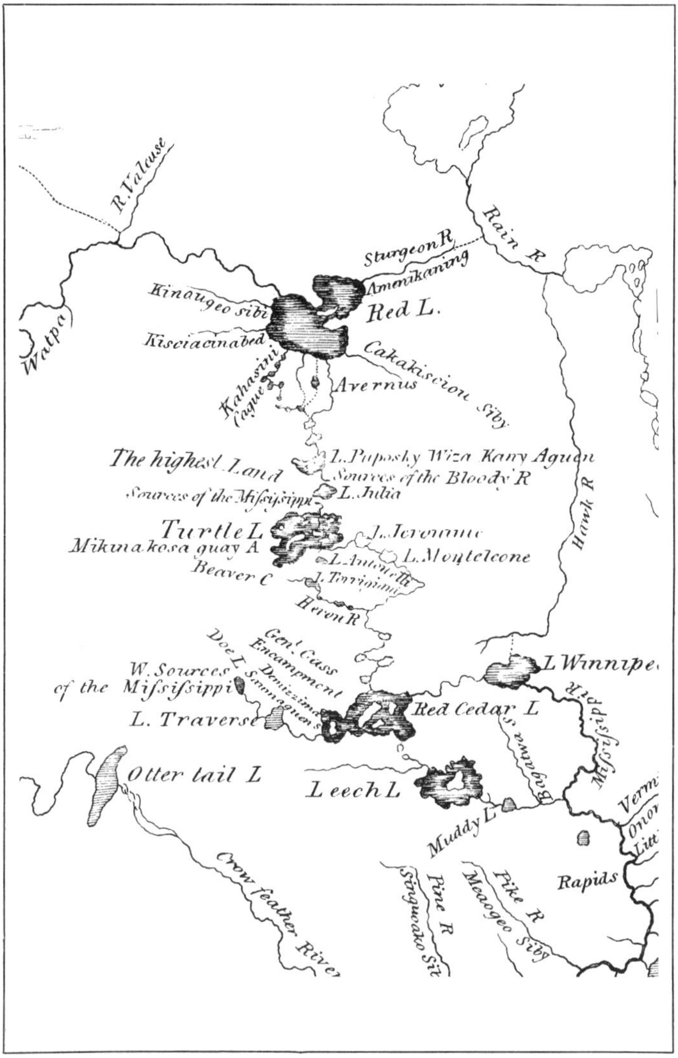

Map of Lake Julia and Lake LaBiche—Itasca. Beltrami, although he did not travel to Lake LaBiche (Doe Lake), which Henry Schoolcraft later called Itasca, indicated on his map that he considered it the Western Sources of the Mississippi, albeit secondary to Lake Julia.

Before 1803, there is no record that anyone other than Indians had visited the headwaters now considered as the source of the Mississippi River. A fur trader named William Morrison was perhaps the first explorer in the region of Lake Itasca. As early as 1803, and subsequently, Morrison kept a journal of his movements. All his notes were lost, however, when his canoe capsized, but later his daughter recalled her father's vivid accounts of his travels in the region. Apparently, Morrison voiced no ideas at the time as to the lake as the source of the Mississippi.[6]

In the light of contemporary information, Beltrami's boast that he had discovered the Mississippi's northernmost source at the lake he named for the Countess Giulia Spada de Medici was not an irresponsible claim, whatever subsequent exploration demonstrated. Beltrami, who had crossed the watershed from the north, saw water trickling both north and south from Lake Julia. And he was convinced that he had discovered the ultimate source of the Mississippi, tracing the flow from Lake Julia through the swampy area to Turtle Lake and thence to Turtle River.

The Minnesota Historical Society in 1889 set up a commission to investigate all claims as to the true source of the Mississippi River. The commission's findings were based on the theory that the source of a river is to be found in the "most remote watershed from its mouth." It concluded, therefore, that the Itasca basin was such a watershed for the Mississippi. It also concluded that Joseph N. Nicollet had discovered in 1836 the longest and largest stream within the Itasca basin and that William Morrison in 1804, H. R. Schoolcraft in 1832 and Nicollet in 1836 "were the first white men to discover the sources of the Mississippi." [7]

It is ironic that Beltrami, who was within several days journey of Lake Itasca, recognized it as a source of the

Mississippi but decided it was unnecessary for him to go there because of his conviction that Lake Julia was the river's main source.

Although the Minnesota Historical Society's commission designated the Itasca basin as the most remote source of the Mississippi, it did not apply the principle to the Missouri River, which rises in the Rocky Mountains 3,700 miles from the Mississippi's mouth.

Joseph N. Nicollet, an astronomer and mathematician, was the only true scientist involved in searching for the Mississippi's source in an expedition in 1836. Whereas Beltrami, neither an explorer nor geographer, but, in his words, "a solitary pilgrim—a rambler," ventured into the wilderness unequipped with scientific instruments, Nicollet took with him all the paraphernalia necessary for a scientific survey—sextant, barometer, thermometer, chronometer, compass, artificial horizon, tape line and other accessories.[8]

Nicollet had read Beltrami's *Découverte* and did not find himself among those critics who dismissed the Italian lightly. "I may be mistaken," he wrote, "but it strikes me that American critics have been too disdainful of Mr. Beltrami's book . . . My opinion is, that it deserved a critical review and a severe refutation." [9] In brief, Nicollet was saying that serious arguments rather than scornful treatment, should have been directed against Beltrami, his book and his claims.

From the perspective of nearly 150 years and with the fact always in mind that Beltrami, without scientific equipment or experience as an explorer, penetrated the wilderness alone, the Italian does not show up badly in the quest to discover the source of the Mississippi.

A romantic traveler, ever curious for knowledge and ever avid for adventure, Beltrami nonetheless exhibited as much courage, endurance, dedication and determination as the handful who preceded him and those that followed.

One historian has called Beltrami "perhaps the most picturesque and unique figure in the series of many explorers of the area of Minnesota." [10]

Beltrami was one of the first to describe the beautiful valley of the Minnesota River, the plains of the Red River of the North, the Red Lake region, Turtle Lake and River, and the epic journey of the first steamboat trip of the *Virginia* to Fort St. Anthony. He provided a detailed map of the course of his travels. Beltrami's map identified La Biche Lake south-southwest of Turtle Lake, whereas Schoolcraft in his 1821 map, incorrectly indicated La Biche Lake as west-northwest of Turtle Lake. Beltrami described accurately the life, customs, rites, of the Indians and the flora and fauna of the territory which he crossed.

Moreover, Beltrami accomplished his difficult and fantastic journey relying only upon his own resources, most of the time alone.

No one need, or indeed, can, diminish the accomplishments of the several explorers who sought the elusive source of the Mississippi. Nor should one exclude Beltrami from an honorable place among them. He earned a greater recognition than history has bestowed upon him. The unfair, unkind, and even malicious criticism during his stay in America and England was undeserved. Perhaps his contemporaries viewed Beltrami as a traveler who trespassed on the private preserve of another nation without authorization; perhaps there was no room for a "foreigner" and an amateur traveler in the folklore of the exploration of the Mississippi Valley. However, the recognition given by the State of Minnesota and the Minnesota Historical Society in 1866 proves that if such an attitude existed, it did not continue for as long as half a century.

How strange appears this sentimental wanderer in the Indian Country—amidst the intrigues to control the fur trade, among political agents serving selfish aims, among exploiters of immigrants, and whiskey dispensers debauching the Indians. The era was overwhelmingly anti-Indian and unsympathetic to those who defended their rights. Beltrami was such a defender.

One of the most apt and truest appraisals of Giacomo Costantino Beltrami comes from the pen of a modern historian. "While undoubtedly grandiose, vainglorious, and sometimes ridiculous, yet he was also gallant, brave and adventurous," wrote Edward C. Gale. "He rode across the Minnesota horizon like some armored knight clad in the mental panoply of the Middle Ages, to which period he really belonged." [11]

NOTES

CHAPTER ONE

1. J. C. [Giacomo Costantino] Beltrami, *A Pilgrimage in Europe and America* (2 Vols. London, 1828), I, 471–472. Hereafter cited as Beltrami, *A Pilgrimage*. Volume II, *A Pilgrimage in America*, is available in an American edition (Chicago, 1962).

2. J. C. Beltrami, *Deux Mots sur des Promenades de Paris à Liverpool* (Philadelphia, 1823). Hereafter cited as Beltrami, *Deux Mots*.

3. J. C. Beltrami, *La Découverte des Sources du Mississippi et de la Rivière Sanglante* (New Orleans, 1824). Hereafter cited as Beltrami, *La Découverte*.

4. J. C. Beltrami, *Le Mexique* (2 Vols.; Paris, 1830).

5. Beltrami, *A Pilgrimage*, II, 474.

CHAPTER TWO

1. Wally Braghieri Giacomini, *Giacomo Costantino Beltrami* (Bergamo, 1955), 21–22. Hereafter cited as Giacomini, *Beltrami*. Eugenia Masi, *Giacomo Costantino Beltrami* (Florence, 1902), 1–3. Hereafter cited as Masi, *Beltrami*.

2. Ferdinando Martini, *Donne, Salotti e Costumi—La Vita Italiana* (Milan, 1931), 339–43.

3. Giacomini, *Beltrami*, 23–24; Masi, *Beltrami*, 4–8.

4. Silvio Zavatti, "La Persecuzione di Costantino Beltrami," *Giornale di Bergamo*, November 10, 1968, p. 15.

5. Giacomini, *Beltrami*, 23–24; Masi, *Beltrami*, 7–8.

6. Countess d'Albany to Beltrami, April 7, 1818; in Beltrami Collection, Biblioteca Civica, Bergamo.

7. Giacomini, *Beltrami*, 25; Masi, *Beltrami*, 12–13.
8. *Enciclopedia Italiana Treccani* (Milan, 1929–39). Articles "Risorgimento," "Carboneria," "Italia."
9. Beltrami, *Le Mexique*, II, 314–16.
10. Beltrami, *A Pilgrimage*, I, xxvi; 2.
11. Jack F. Bernard, *Up from Caesar* (Garden City, N.Y., 1970), 348.
12. Beltrami, *A Pilgrimage*, I, 30, 59.
13. Beltrami's Passport, in Beltrami Collection, Bergamo.

CHAPTER THREE

1. All the information in this Chapter is based on Beltrami, *A Pilgrimage*, (1828 London Edition), Vol. I, Pages 80–270. His tastes, ideas, prejudices and the characteristics of his personality are reflected in Beltrami's text.

CHAPTER FOUR

1. Beltrami, *A Pilgrimage*, I, 280.
2. Beltrami, *A Pilgrimage*, I, 277–78.
3. Beltrami, *A Pilgrimage*, I, 285–286.
4. Beltrami, *A Pilgrimage*, I, 300–301.
5. Beltrami, *A Pilgrimage*, I, 304.
6. Beltrami, *A Pilgrimage*, I, 307–308.
7. Beltrami, *A Pilgrimage*, I, 328–331.
8. Beltrami, *A Pilgrimage*, I, 468–471, 332, 333, 339, 341; Charles Graves, *Leather Armchairs* (New York, 1964), 35–37.
9. Beltrami, *A Pilgrimage*, I, 342, 344, 345.
10. Beltrami, *A Pilgrimage*, I, 351–352, 348, 357, 353–354, 357–358, 389, 392.
11. Beltrami, *A Pilgrimage*, I, 461–465.
12. Glasgow *Scots Times*, February 16, 1828; London *Quarterly Review*, LXXIV (April 4, 1828), 450.
13. Beltrami, *A Pilgrimage*, I, 349.
14. Beltrami is notoriously unreliable on dates. He wrote (*A Pilgrimage*, II, 3): "We left Prince's dock on the 3rd of November." Yet, in *Deux Mots*, published on his arrival in Philadelphia, he states his departure from Liverpool was October 27.

The Liverpool *Mercury*, November 1, 1822, reported that the *Reaper* had sailed on October 25 for Philadelphia. The *Reaper* arrived in that city on December 30, 1822, and reported having made the crossing in sixty days.

The *National Gazette* of Philadelphia, on December 30, 1822, reported the arrival of the "Ship *Reaper* [(Captain] Winnemore)—Liverpool—60 days . . . Passengers: General Costantine Beltrome [sic] and two in steerage." A transcript prepared by the United States Department of State, *Passengers Who Arrived in the United States September 1821–December 1823* (Baltimore, 1969, p. 194), lists December 31, 1822, "Jas. C. Dettrone [*sic*]—age 42—Male—from Italy—ship, Reaper."

15. Beltrami, *A Pilgrimage*, II, 30.
16. Beltrami, *A Pilgrimage*, I, 471–472.

CHAPTER FIVE

1. Beltrami, *A Pilgrimage*, II, 55–56.
2. J. B. Tasca to Beltrami, March 28, 1823, in Collection of Count Glauco Luchetti, Filottrano; Beltrami, *A Pilgrimage*, II, 49, 33, 44, 45, 48, 58.
3. Beltrami, *A Pilgrimage*, II, 50, 51.
4. Beltrami, *A Pilgrimage*, II, 52.
5. Beltrami, *A Pilgrimage*, II, 56.
6. Beltrami, *A Pilgrimage*, II, 57–58.
7. Beltrami, *A Pilgrimage*, II, 62–64.
8. Beltrami, *A Pilgrimage*, II, 67–101. The Italian's descriptions of the Ohio River, its towns and steamboats are detailed.

CHAPTER SIX

1. Alfred J. Hill, "Constantine Beltrami," in *Minnesota Historical Society Collections* (St. Paul, 1889), II, 193. Hereafter cited as Hill, "Constantine Beltrami"
2. Beltrami, *A Pilgrimage*, II, 100–101, 126, 105.
3. Major Lawrence Taliaferro was named by President Monroe (a fellow Virginian) as Indian agent at St. Peter near the Falls of St. Anthony. He was then twenty-five years old. Taliaferro had volunteered for the War of 1812 at the age of eighteen and at the end of the war was commissioned a Lieutenant in the regular army. In the next two decades he was to become a very influential person in the affairs of the upper Mississippi. From Fort Snelling the jurisdiction of his agency extended to embrace both the Sioux and the Chippewa nations. The Indians respected him, as he had earned their confidence by being entirely truthful with them. Taliaferro was known to the Indians as *Mahsabusca* ("Iron Cutter," the translation of his name). It is interesting to note that he gave his servant girl

Harriet Robinson in marriage to Dred Scott, the plaintiff in the famous legal case, and that he himself performed the ceremony. Later he emancipated all of his slaves at a time when they were worth some thirty thousand dollars. Taliaferro was of a proud bearing, which could be mistaken for arrogance. It was to his credit that he was cordially hated by all who could not bribe him or frighten him in his duties to defend the Indians from the abuses of the Indian traders and speculators. He received six successive appointments for his agency from four different Presidents. It was a high tribute to a man scrupulously honest and incorruptible. He resigned his position and left the upper Mississippi in 1839. William Watts Folwell, *A History of Minnesota* (St. Paul, 1956), I, 140–143. Hereafter cited as Folwell, *Minnesota.*

4. Hill, "Constantine Beltrami," 192.

5. Beltrami, *A Pilgrimage*, II, 124.

6. The *Missouri Republican* (St. Louis), April 23, 1823 reported the *Virginia* departure from St. Louis for St. Peter on Monday, April 21, 1823. Characteristically, Beltrami recorded the date incorrectly. In the French edition (1824) of his travels, he gives the date as April 6; in the English edition (1828) as May 2.

7. In answering a reviewer of *A Pilgrimage in Europe and America* in the London *Quarterly Review* in 1828, Beltrami corrected this obvious mistake. He wrote, "I hope that the least attentive reader will have noticed that the first error, '*twenty-two thousand miles*,' ought to be printed 'two thousand two hundred miles,' as the length of the steamboat's course up the Mississippi." *Beltrami's "Pilgrimage," and the Quarterly Review* (London, 1828).

8. Beltrami, *A Pilgrimage*, II, 128–153. Description of voyage of Virginia and Beltrami's first encounter with Indians.

9. Beltrami, *A Pilgrimage*, II, 154, 159, 188, 177.

10. "Auto-Biography of Major Lawrence Taliaferro—Written in 1864," *Minnesota Historical Society Collections* (St. Paul, 1894), VI, 240, 241.

11. Beltrami, *A Pilgrimage*, II, 161.

12. William J. Petersen, "The 'Virginia,' the 'Clermont' of the Upper Mississippi," *Minnesota Historical Society Quarterly Magazine*, IX (1928), 347–62; Fred A. Bill, "History of Early Steamboat Navigation on River," Wabasha *County Herald*, July 10, 1924. Beltrami, *A Pilgrimage*, II, 196–197. Subsequent measurements proved that Beltrami erred when he gave the distance as 925 miles. A survey made by U. S. Engineers in 1888 established the distance as 729 miles. George B. Merrick, *Old Times on the Upper Mississippi* (Cleveland 1909), Appendix C, 298. The *Virginia* made a second trip to Fort St. Anthony (May 27–June 12) and was lost on Septem-

ber 19, 1823, when it struck a snag on its way from Louisville to St. Louis. *Niles' Weekly Register*, XXV (October 11, 1823), 95.

13. Beltrami, *A Pilgrimage*, II, 199–200.

CHAPTER SEVEN

1. Donald Jackson (ed.), *The Journal of Zebulon Montgomery Pike* (Norman, Okla., 1966), 246, 247; Folwell, *Minnesota*, I, 92, 93, 94; Lawrence Taliaferro, Journal (MS in Minnesota Historical Society, St. Paul), June 22, October 11, 12, 14, 15, 1838.

2. Colonel Josiah Snelling was born in Boston in 1782. He was commissioned a first lieutenant of Infantry in 1808, was promoted to captain the following year, and participated in the War of 1812. He was breveted major for gallantry in August, 1812. At the end of the War of 1812, his rank was lieutenant colonel and in 1819 was assigned to the Fifth Infantry as colonel. During the seven years of his command at Fort St. Anthony, he fulfilled his duties with ability, prudence, and courage. The War Department in 1825 changed the name of Fort St. Anthony to Fort Snelling. He died in 1828 at the age of 45.

3. Evan Jones, *Citadel in the Wilderness* (New York, 1966), 48, 49, 50. Hereafter cited as Jones, *Citadel*; Marilyn Ziebarth and Alan Ominsky, *Fort Snelling: Anchor Post of the Northwest* (St. Paul, Minn., 1970).

4. Beltrami, *A Pilgrimage*, II, 201–203.

5. Elizabeth F. Ellet, *Pioneer Women of the West* (Philadelphia, 1852), 327. Beltrami "brought letters of introduction from Mrs. Snelling's friends in St. Louis. The colonel invited him to his house to remain as long as he pleased." Hereafter cited as Ellet, *Pioneer Women*.

6. Beltrami, *A Pilgrimage*, II, 194.

7. Ellet, *Pioneer Women*, 328.

8. William H. Keating, *Narrative of an Expedition* (Minneapolis, 1959), II, 305. The 2-volume book was first published in Philadelphia in 1824. All references are from the 1959 reprint edition unless otherwise noted. Hereafter cited as Keating, *Narrative*.

9. Jones, *Citadel*, 75.

10. Ellet, *Pioneer Women*, 328.

11. Evan Jones, *The Minnesota: Forgotten River* (New York, 1962), 69, 70.

12. Beltrami, *A Pilgrimage*, II, 233–234.

13. Beltrami, *A Pilgrimage*, II, 239–240; Passport in Beltrami Collection, Bergamo.

14. Beltrami, *A Pilgrimage,* II, 301–304.

15. Major Stephen H. Long *Diary,* entry of July 9, 1823. Manuscript in collection of Minnesota Historical Society. Hereafter cited as Long, *Diary.*

CHAPTER EIGHT

1. Dr. Thomas Say (1787–1834) has been called the father of descriptive entomology.

2. Joseph Renville was born about 1779, the son of a Sioux woman and a French fur trader. Shrewdly intelligent, Renville was imperious and knew his power. With the Indian and half-breed his word was law. During the War of 1812 Renville commanded a detachment of Sioux and held the rank of captain in the British army. In 1822 he established himself near the junction of Lac Qui Parle and the Minnesota River. Here he built a long stockage known as Fort Renville and lived in patriarchal splendor. The State of Minnesota later honored this great guide by naming a county for him, as it also did for Beltrami.

3. Keating, *Narrative,* I, 3, 4, 327.

4. Keating, *Narrative,* I, 328, 339.

5. Beltrami, *A Pilgrimage,* II, 304–305, 307–309, 311–314, 317–318, 321–323.

6. Keating, *Narrative,* I, 378; II, 216–217; Beltrami, *A Pilgrimage,* II, 323–324.

7. Keating, *Narrative,* I, 445; Beltrami, *A Pilgrimage,* II, 323.

8. Beltrami, *A Pilgrimage,* II, 325–326; Keating, *Narrative,* I, 455–456.

9. Beltrami, *A Pilgrimage,* II, 327, 329–331.

10. Beltrami, *A Pilgrimage,* II, 333, 335–337.

11. Keating, *Narrative,* II, 12–16.

12. Beltrami, *A Pilgrimage,* II, 346–347; Keating, *Narrative,* II, 32, 43.

13. Long *Diary.*

14. Beltrami, *A Pilgrimage,* 369, 357, 370.

15. Beltrami, *A Pilgrimage,* 369.

CHAPTER NINE

1. This Chapter is based on material found in Beltrami, *A Pilgrimage,* II, 369–397.

CHAPTER TEN

1. Beltrami, *A Pilgrimage,* II, 403, 405. Joseph N. Nicollet (1786–1843), the eminent Savoyard astronomer and geographer, who made a survey of the hydrographical basin of the Upper Mississippi River in 1836–40, showed in his map published in 1843 that the Red Lake River entering the Red Lake from the southeast and flowing out from the west side.

2. Beltrami, *A Pilgrimage,* II, 401–402. Beltrami does not name the family from which he drew the names Alexander, Lavinius, Everard, Frederica, Adela, Magdalena, Virginia, and Eleonora.

3. Beltrami, *A Pilgrimage,* II, 406–409.

4. Beltrami, *A Pilgrimage,* II, 410–415.

5. Beltrami, Passport in Beltrami Collection, Bergamo. The poem bearing the notation "At the source of the Mississippi—August 31, 1823," translated reads:

> Fame that records the glorious names
> And divulges their labors and great deeds,
> Fly and tell to all you meet, Sbirri and Kings,
> That here I reign alone and alone sojourn,
> That Alcandro here first put his foot
> And to him my will gives precedence.

Alcandro Grineo was the poetical name given to Beltrami by the Accademia dei Catenati of Macerata.

6. Beltrami, *A Pilgrimage,* II, 416–418, 405; David Thompson, *Thompson's Narrative, 1784–1812,* ed. Richard Glover, (Toronto, 1962): Hereafter cited as Thompson, *Narrative.* "By 9 P M on the 23rd of April we had carried all over, and now had to cross the country to the Turtle Lake, the head of the Mississippi River . . ." wrote Thompson. In Thompson's notes there is this reference to Turtle brook: "This is the source of the famous Mississippi in the most direct line. All of the other little sources are reckoned to be subordinate to this, as they are longer in forming so considerable a stream." Thompson was born in London in 1770, went to Western Canada in 1784 as an apprentice to the Hudson's Bay Company. During his career as a fur trader for this company, Thompson kept careful journals and field notes of his travels. In 1844, he prepared the *Narrative.* It was first published in 1888. Thompson died in Canada in 1857.

7. Beltrami, *A Pilgrimage,* II, 419–421, 423–429, 430–435; Beltrami, *La Découverte,* 257–58.

8. Beltrami, *A Pilgrimage,* II, 438–441, 446–448, 450–451.

9. Beltrami, *A Pilgrimage,* II, 451; John Upton Terrell, *Furs by Astor* (New York, 1963), 272–273.

10. Beltrami, *A Pilgrimage,* II, 450–451, 460–461.

11. Taliaferro, "Auto-Biography," 241–242; Beltrami, *A Pilgrimage*, II, 480–483; 484–486.

12. Beltrami, *A Pilgrimage*, II, 489–491; Major Taliaferro's Journal contains the following entries: "September 15, [1823] Mr. Beltrami arrived this day from the sources of the Mississippi, in company with forty or fifty Chippewas." And on "September 25, [1823] Mr. Beltrami left this [sic] for Italy this morning." Beltrami, as usual was unreliable in his dates and he gives September 29 as date of his arrival at Fort St. Anthony and October 3 as his date of departure.

CHAPTER ELEVEN

1. New Orleans *Courrier de la Louisiane*, December 15, 1823; Beltrami, *A Pilgrimage*, II, 492.

2. Beltrami, *A Pilgrimage*, II, 499–500, 495, 541–542.

3. Beltrami, *A Pilgrimage*, II, 503, 509, 516, 520–521.

4. New Orleans *Louisiana Gazette*, December 15, 1823; *Courrier de la Louisiane*, December 15, 1823.

5. Beltrami, *A Pilgrimage*, II, 522–23. In the 1820 census, the total population is listed as 29,000. John Paxton, who published the *New Orleans Directory and Register* for 1822, estimates that 40,000 would be more accurate. Generally a great many new Orleanians were out of the city in the summer on account of yellow fever, when the census was taken. In view of these facts, Beltrami's estimate of 45,000 seems reasonably accurate.

6. John Adems Paxton, *The New Orleans Directory and Register* (New Orleans, 1822, 1823, 1824); Beltrami, *A Pilgrimage*, II, 524–26; S. Croce and David H. Wallace, *The New York Historical Society Dictionary of Artists in America*, 1564–1860 (New Haven, 1957); *Louisiana Gazette*, January 3, January 7, January 13, 1824. See also, *Louisiana Gazette* and *Courrier de la Louisiane* for January, February, March, April, 1824.

7. Beltrami, *A Pilgrimage*, II, 542; Roger Baudier, *The Catholic Church in Louisiana* (New Orleans, 1939), 254, 269, 275–76. Père Antoine was one of the most extraordinary figures of this era in New Orleans. He was pastor of the St. Louis Cathedral and remained in that position until his death despite the opposition of his own superiors and of the Bishop of New Orleans. (Bishop Dubourg had petitioned Rome for permission to move his residence to St. Louis away from "that wretched Religious.") In the face of such hostility, Père Antoine remained a charitable man. Admirers and friends gave him large sums of money, which he used for alms to the poor and to embellish the cathedral. He was particularly kind to children. Never

a stern disciplinarian, Père Antoine appeared to have had love and compassion for everyone. He gave the rites and blessings of the Catholic Church to all that came to him, and even held Masonic funerals in the cathedral with full insignia and paraphernalia on the coffin. Many of his admirers and followers abused his kindness and sometimes naiveté, but they were completely devoted to him and supported him as a pastor of the cathedral.

8. Beltrami, *A Pilgrimage in America,* 531–533. After the British departure from New Orleans, rumors of a peace treaty began to reach the city. Lacking official information, General Jackson considered the rumor to be a maneuver of British secret agents in New Orleans to create discord and give a false sense of security. Many French citizens, who had fought at Chalmette, obtained their discharge, through the office of the French Consul. General Jackson then ordered all such Frenchmen to remove themselves from the city within three days. On March 3, 1815, the Louisiana Courrier carried an unsigned letter to the editor bitterly criticizing Jackson's order. Jackson learned that the writer was Louis Louallier, a member of the Louisiana Legislature, and immediately ordered his arrest. Federal Judge Dominick A. Hall issued a writ of habeas corpus for the release of Louallier and General Jackson, incensed at Judge Hall's action, had the jurist arrested on March 11 and escorted out of the city.

On March 13, a courier from Washington brought official news of the ratification of the Treaty of Ghent. Jackson ended martial law in New Orleans and Judge Hall returned to the city. Immediately he cited Jackson for contempt of court, and fined him $1,000, a fine which General Jackson, appearing in court in civilian clothes, promptly paid.

By Act of Congress of February 16, 1844, the fine was remitted with interest.

9. Beltrami deposited a copy of his book with and had its title registered by the Clerk of the United States District Court for the Eastern District of Louisiana, which issued an official certificate dated March 14, 1824, to that effect. *Le Courrier de la Louisiane, L'Ami des Lois,* April 12, 1824.

10. Joseph F. Carronge to Beltrami, April 13, 1824; Horatio Davis to Beltrami, April 12, 1824; Mayor Louis Roffignac to Beltrami, April 10, 1824; Governor Thomas B. Robertson to Beltrami, April 21, 1824. All in Beltrami Collection in Bergamo.

11. *Courrier de la Louisiane,* April 15, 1824; New Orleans *Argus,* April 21, 1824; *Louisiana Gazette,* April 23, 1824.

12. *Argus,* April 20, 1824.

13. Beltrami, *Le Mexique,* I, 2–7, 12. This work, published in French, has not been translated into English and is virtually unknown in Mexico. *Le Mexique* exists only in the 1830 Paris edition.

14. He was listed as "James Costantin Bettrani" on the passenger list of the *Sally Ann*, arriving April 27, 1825, in *Passenger List of Ships Entering New Orleans*, 1813–37 (MS in Louisiana State Museum Library, New Orleans).

15. *Courrier de la Louisiane*, May 3, 1825. Beltrami's most valuable discoveries were fourteen painted tablets on agave papyrus assembled as a book. These paintings represented the fourteen epochs of the Aztec dynasty to Montezuma and the Spanish conquest. The Franciscan friar Motolinia (Toribio de Bonavente), sensing their historical value, had saved the tablets from burning when the invading Spaniards destroyed all ancient religious symbols. (Beltrami, *Le Mexique*, II, 86, 87.) In a convent, Beltrami had also discovered a volume of 250 folios containing the original manuscript of the gospels in the Aztec language, translated in 1532 by Friar Bernardino of Sahagum (Bernardino Ribeirà). (Beltrami, *Le Mexique*, II, 168–175.)

CHAPTER TWELVE

1. Keating, *Narrative*, I, p. xvii.
2. Keating, *Narrative*, (Philadelphia, 1824), I, 314–315 n.
3. H. C. Carey and I. Lea to Beltrami, July 15, 1825, in Beltrami Collection, Bergamo.
4. William H. Keating to Beltrami, July 15, 1825, Beltrami Collection, Bergamo.
5. Beltrami to Stephen H. Long, July 19, 1825, (copy) in Beltrami Collection, Bergamo.
6. Keating, *Narrative*, I, 327.
7. New York *Commercial Advertiser*, July 29, 1825.
8. Robert Walsh, Jr. (1784–1859) had traveled in France and the British isles and had contributed to the Paris press and to the *Edinburgh Review*. On returning to America, Walsh settled in Philadelphia, where he founded the *National Gazette*, and served as its editor for fifteen years. He founded the *American Quarterly Review*, which he directed for ten years. In 1812 he was elected to membership in the American Philosophical Society.
9. Beltrami to Robert Walsh, Jr., July 28, 1825, (copy), in Beltrami Collection, Bergamo.
10. Richard G. Wood, *Stephen Harriman Long, 1784–1864* (Glendale, Calif., 1966), 237; Long was born in Hopkinton, N. H., on December 30, 1784. He was graduated from Dartmouth College in 1809 and in 1814 entered the army as second lieutenant of engineers. After serving two years as assistant professor of mathematics at West Point, he was transferred to the topographical engineers

with the rank of major. In 1817 the War Department sent him west to explore the Mississippi. Long's account of this expedition is *Voyage in a Six-oared Skiff to the Falls of Saint Anthony in 1817* (Philadelphia, 1860). In 1819 he was sent on an expedition to the Rocky Mountains. He reached the Rockies in July, 1820. A narrative of this journey is given in James, *Account of an Expedition from Pittsburgh to the Rocky Mountains.* In 1823 Long was assigned to explore the source of the St. Peter (Minnesota) River and the northern boundary of the United States to the Great Lakes. In 1827 the War Department appointed Long to act as consulting engineer for the Baltimore-Ohio Railroad Company. Continued friction with the management of the company led him to withdraw all connection with it. In 1829 he published the first *Rail Road Manual* in the United States. In 1861 he became chief of the Corps of Engineers with rank of a colonel. He died in 1864.

CHAPTER THIRTEEN

1. Giacomo Costantino Beltramo, *To the Public of New York and of the United States,* reprinted in *Magazine of History,* XL (1930), 173–202. Hereafter cited as Beltrami, *To the Public.*

2. Beltrami, *To the Public,* 176–77.

3. Beltrami's Passport in Beltrami Collection, Bergamo; Beltrami, *Le Mexique,* I, 27–28.

4. *London Magazine,* March, 1827, 401–406. Beltrami, *Le Mexique,* I, xv.

5. London *Weekly Review,* December 29, 1827, 481–484; London *Literary Chronicle,* Feb. (?), 1828; *Monthly Review,* February 1828, 250–256; London *Times,* February 11, 1828; Glasgow *Scots Times,* February 16, 1328; London *Atlas,* January 20, 1828; London *Examiner,* February 10, 1828, *Le Furet de Londres,* February (?), 1828. All these extracts are in Beltrami Collection in Bergamo.

6. *Quarterly Review,* LXXIV (1828), 448–458.

7. Giacomo Costantino Beltrami, *Beltrami's "Pilgrimage," and the Quarterly Review,* 1, 2, 15.

CHAPTER FOURTEEN

1. François Auguste René Chateaubriand, *Voyage en Amérique.* (1828), 37–38. Hereafter cited as Chateaubriand, *Voyage.*

2. *Foreign Review and Continental Miscellany,* I, (1828), 470–71.

3. Ernest Dick, *Plagiats de Chateaubriand, le Voyage en Amérique* (Berne, 1905), 5–53.

4. Chateaubriand, *Voyage*, 38–39, 133, 199–200. The months of the year in the Sioux and Chippewa languages listed in *La Découverte* were reproduced and Chateaubriand credited a "*voyageur moderne*." Several paragraphs praising the work of the French missionaries in new France, which appeared in Beltrami's book, also were used in the *Voyage* with due credit; Beltrami, *Le Mexique*, I, p. xx.; Chateaubriand to Beltrami, June 22, 1829, in Beltrami Collection, Bergamo.

5. Joseph Bédier, *Chateaubrand en Amérique: Verité et Fiction* (Paris, 1900), 19–20, 34, 77, n.; George Washington, *Writings*, Bicentennial Edition, XXXI (1939), 355; "Works of Chateaubriand," *American Quarterly Review*, (1827), 460.

CHAPTER FIFTEEN

1. Certificates of Membership Société de Géographie, June 22, 1829; Institute Historique, May 15, 1834; Société Universelle de Civilisation, March 21, 1833; Société Géologique de France, July 16, 1832; all in Beltrami Collection in Bergamo.

2. Hill, "Constantine Beltrami," II, 190.

3. Giacomo Costantino Beltrami, *L' Italie et l'Europe* (Paris, 1834).

4. Beltrami to Monsieur Monglave, Secretary of the Historical Institute of France, February 17, 1836, in Beltrami Collection, Bergano; Beltrami to the President of Académie des Sciences, July 2, 1837, in Beltrami Collection, Bergamo.

5. Beltrami's Will (MS in Notarial Archives of Giuseppe Pellegrini, Macerata). A copy of the will is also in the Dante Alighieri Society in Rome.

6. The Italian historian Gabriele Rosa was elected to honorary membership in the Minnesota Historical Society in 1864; Beltrami manuscripts, letters, documents, passports, newspapers, and certificates are now deposited in the Biblioteca Civica in Bergamo. The Indian memorabilia and artifacts, the clothing worn by Beltrami in his expedition, and the red silk umbrella are now in the Museo di Scienze Naturali in Bergamo; the portrait of Beltrami by Enrico Scuri (1806–1884), originally in the Carrara Academy, is now in the Museo di Scienze Naturali in Bergamo.

7. Alfred James Hill (1833–95) was born in London. In 1854 he emigrated to America and settled in Minnesota. A surveyor and draftsman, he became interested in historical and geographical researches, contributing significantly to the collections of the Minne-

sota Historical Society. It was he who "discovered" Beltrami for Minnesota.

8. Hill to Mayor of Bergamo, July 9, 1863, in Beltrami Collection, Bergamo; Camozzi Vertova, *Notizie e Lettere* (1865); Minutes of Executive Council Meeting, February 12, 1866 (MS in Minnesota Historical Society, St. Paul); *Journal of the House of Representatives of Minnesota,* 8th Sess., February 20, 1866. *Minnesota Laws, 1866,* Chap. 46, constituting County of Beltrami.

9. Henry Hastings Sibley (1811–1891), Minnesota pioneer and politician, an agent of the America Fur Company, established himself at Mendota, near Fort Snelling, in 1835. He was a prominent figure in Minnesota until his death in 1891; Henry Hastings Sibley to Camozzi Vertova, March 6, 1867, in Beltrami Collection, Bergamo.

CHAPTER SIXTEEN

1. Thompson, *Narrative,* 1784–1812, 200 n 1.

2. Zebulon M. Pike, *The Journals, with Letters and Documents,* ed. Donald Jackson (Norman, Okla., 1966), I, 87, 88. Zebulon M. Pike was born in Lamberton, New Jersey, on January 5, 1779. At the age of fifteen Zebulon enlisted in his father's military company. He spent much of his early career on the Ohio and Mississippi rivers. In 1805, he was directed to explore the Mississippi to its source. Later Pike explored the headwaters of the Arkansas and Red rivers. In the attack on York (now Toronto) in the War of 1812, Pike, a brigadier general, was killed. He was thirty-four.

3. Henry R. Schoolcraft, *Narrative Journal of Travels,* ed. Mentor L. Williams (East Lansing, Mich., 1853), 168–69.

4. Philip P. Mason, ed., *Schoolcraft's Expedition to Lake Itasca: The Discovery of the Source of the Mississippi* (East Lansing, Mich., 1958), 25, 35, 205, 286, n 2, 350–351. Henry Rowe Schoolcraft was born in Albany, New York, in 1793. At the age of twenty-four he went to the Northwest in search of fame and fortune. He was a mineralogist, Indian agent, an expert in the Chippewa language and folklore, an author, a writer of poetry, a politician, and most of all a talented and ambitious opportunist. He first received public notice upon the publication of his book about a journey to the lead mines of Missouri. In 1823 he married Jane Johnston, the daughter of a prominent fur trader of Sault Ste. Marie. Her mother was the daughter of a powerful Chippewa chief, Waub Ojeeg. Jane Schoolcraft's knowledge of Indian customs, legends, and languages and her contacts through her mother's relatives were invaluable to her husband. This made Schoolcraft a recognized authority on the

Chippewa Indians. He participated in the politics of the territory of Michigan and was elected to the legislature from 1828 to 1832. He became a leader in the educational and cultural life of the territory.

His *Narrative Journal . . . to the Sources of the Mississippi River* appeared in 1821. In 1834 his *Narrative of an Expedition Through the Upper Mississippi to Itasca Lake, the Actual Source of the Mississippi* was issued. He promoted the study of Indian ethnology, both at home and abroad, and wrote many books on this subject. He died on December 10, 1864.

5. Beltrami, *La Découverte,* 257; Beltrami, *A Pilgrimage,* II, 405–406.

6. Jacob V. Brower, *The Mississippi River and Its Source* (Minneapolis, 1893), 119–24. Hereafter cited as Brower, *The Mississippi*; William Morrison, letter under title "Who Discovered Itasca Lake?" Minnesota Historical Society Collections, I (1872), 417–19.

7. Brower, *The Mississippi,* 294–295, 297–301. The Royal Geographic Society of England, when asked for a definition of the source of a river, answered that "it has never laid down any rule defining what constitutes the source of a river." Professor W. M. Davis of Harvard University answered that he was inclined to follow the longest surface channel as the source of a river.

8. E. D. Neill, "Occurrences in and Around Fort Snelling" *Minnesota Historical Society Collections* (St. Paul, 1865), II, 44–45; Taliaferro Journal, July 12, 1830. Joseph N. Nicollet was born in 1786 in Cluses, Savoy. He became a naturalized citizen of France in 1817; but, after financial reverses, he left France for the United States, arriving in New Orleans in 1832. He visited the upper part of the former French Louisiana in St. Louis and became intimate with the influential Chouteau family. His first expedition took place in 1836 to Lake La Biche. In 1838 Nicollet's work came to the attention of Washington officials. He was commissioned, with Lieutenant John C. Fremont as his assistant, to survey the vast region lying between the upper Mississippi and Missouri rivers. After three years of work his map was completed. Nicollet died in Baltimore in 1843.

9. *House Documents,* 28th Cong., 2nd Sess., No. 52, 59.

10. Warren Upham, *Minnesota in Three Centuries,* 1655–1908 (St. Paul, 1908), I, 359.

11. Edward C. Gale, footnote in *The Magazine of History* (Vol. 40, No. 4, 202) (1930) reprint of Beltrami's pamphlet, *To the Public of New York and of the United States.*

BIBLIOGRAPHY

MANUSCRIPTS

Biblioteca Civica, Bergamo:
Giacomo Costantino Beltrami Collection
Biblioteca Comunale, Macerata:
Beltrami Records
Count Glauco Luchetti, Filottrano:
Beltrami Manuscripts
Cabildo Library, New Orleans:
Passenger List of Ships Entering New Orleans, 1813–37.
Minnesota Historical Society, St. Paul:
Lawrence Taliaferro Journal
Stephen Harriman Long Diary

NEWSPAPERS AND JOURNALS

Glasgow *Scots Times,* 1828
Liverpool *Mercury,* 1822
London *Atlas,* 1828
London *Examiner,* 1828
Le Furet de Londres, 1828
London *Literary Chronicle,* 1828
London *Quarterly Review,* 1828
London *Times,* 1828
London *Weekly Review,* 1827
New Orleans *Argus,* 1824

New Orleans *Courrier de la Louisiane,* 1823–25
New Orleans *Louisiana Gazette,* 1823–24
New York *Commercial Advertiser,* 1825
Niles' Weekly Register, 1823
Philadelphia *National Gazette,* 1822–25
St. Louis *Missouri Republican,* 1823

ARTICLES AND BOOKS

Adams, Ann. "Reminiscences of Red River and Fort Snelling." *Minnesota Historical Society Collections,* VI (1894), 75–116.

Angelini, Luigi. "Il Bergamasco Costantino Beltrami alle Sorgenti del Mississippi." *La Martinella di Milano,* X (1956), 484–91.

Armstrong, Emma Kate. "Chateaubriand's America." *Modern Language Association of America,* XXII (1907), 345–70.

Babcock, Willoughby M., Jr. "Major Lawrence Taliaferro, Indian Agent." *Mississippi Valley Historical Review,* XI, (1924), 358–75.

Baker, James H. "The Sources of the Mississippi: Their Discoverer, Real and Pretended." *Minnesota Historical Society Collections,* VI (1887), 3–28.

Baudier, Roger. *The Catholic Church in Louisiana.* New Orleans: 1939.

Bédier, Joseph. *Chateaubriand en Amérique: Vérité et Fiction.* Paris: Colin, 1900.

[Beltrami, Giacomo Costantino.] *Beltrami's "Pilgrimage,"* and the *Quarterly Review.* London: C. H. Reynell, 1828.

Beltrami, J. C. [Giacomo Costantino]. *La Découverte des Sources du Mississippi et de la Rivière Sanglante: Description du Cours du Mississippi, etc.* New Orleans: Benj. Levy, 1824.

_______. *Deux Mots sur des Promenades de Paris à Liverpool.* Philadelphia: I. Ashmead and Co., 1823.

_______. *L'Italie et l'Europe.* Paris: Levrault Delaunay, 1834.

_______. *Le Mexique.* 2 vols. Paris: Crevot, 1830.

_______. *A Pilgrimage in America, Leading to the Discovery of the Sources of the Mississippi and Bloody River; With a Description of the Whole Course of the Former, and of the Ohio.* Chicago: Quadrangle Books, 1962.

_______. *A Pilgrimage in Europe and America, Leading to the Discovery of the Sources of the Mississippi and Bloody River; With a Description of the Whole Course of the Former, and of the Ohio.* 2 vols. London: Hunt and Clarke, 1828.

_______. *To the Public of New York and of the United States.* New York: Joseph Darke, 1825. Reprinted in *Magazine of History,* XL (1930).

Bernard, Jack F. *Up from Caesar.* Garden City, N.Y.: Double-Day and Co., 1970.

Berthel, Mary W. *Minnesota Under Four Flags.* St. Paul: Minnesota Historical Society, 1963.

Bill, Fred A. "History of Early Steamboat Navigation on River." *Wabasha County Herald,* July 10, 1924.

Bliss, John H. "Reminiscences of Fort Snelling." *Minnesota Historical Society Collections,* VI (1894), 335–53.

Brower, Jacob V. *The Mississippi River and Its Sources, Minnesota Historical Collections,* VII. Minneapolis: 1893.

Caruso, John Anthony. *The Mississippi Valley Frontier: The Age of French Exploration and Settlement.* Indianapolis: Bobbs-Merrill Co., 1966.

Chambers, Julius. *The Mississippi River and Its Wonderful Valley.* New York: G. P. Putnam's Sons, 1910.

Chateaubriand, François Auguste René. *Voyage en Amerique: Oeuvres Complétes.* VI. Paris: Pourratt Frères, 1929.

_______. *Mémoires d'Outre Tombe.* I and II. Paris: Gallimard Frères, 1951.

"Chateaubriand's Latest Productions." (Book Review.) *Foreign Review and Continental Miscellany* (London). 1828, pp. 468–89.

Chinard, Gilbert. "Notes sur le Voyage de Chateaubriand en Amérique." *University of California Press,* IV (1915), 269–349.

Christianson, Theodore. "The Long and Beltrami Explorations in Minnesota One Hundred Years Ago." *Minnesota Historical Society Bulletin*, V (1923), 249–64.

Croce, S., and Wallace, David H. *The New York Historical Society Dictionary of Artists in America, 1564–1860*. New Haven: Yale University Press, 1957.

Dick, Ernest. *Les Plagiats de Chateaubriand, Le Voyage en Amérique*. Berne, 1905.

________. "Quelques Sources Ignorées du Voyage en Amérique de Chateaubriand." *Revue d'Histoire Littéraire*, April–June, 1906, pp. 228–45.

Dillon, Richard H. "Stephen Long's Great American Desert." *Proceedings of the American Philosophical Society*, III, No. 2 (1967), 93–108.

Ellet, Elizabeth F. *Pioneer Women of the West*. Philadelphia: Porter and Coats, 1852.

Enciclopedia Italiana Treccani. Milan: Istituto Giovanni Treccani, 1929–39.

Folwell, William Watts. *A History of Minnesota*. 4 vols. St. Paul: Minnesota Historical Society, 1956.

Franzi, Tulli. "Alle Sorgenti del Mississippi." *Rivista di Bergamo*, October, 1926, pp. 3–8.

Ghisleri, Arcangelo. "La Passione dell Esule nei Viaggi di C. Beltrami." *Bergorum*, VII (1928), 326–35.

Giacomini, Wally Braghieri. *Giacomo Costantino Beltrami: Pellegrino Alle Sorgenti del Mississippi*. Bergamo: Edizioni Orobiche, 1855.

Glazier, George H. *Mistakes of Baker: A Reply*. St. Paul, 1887.

Glazier, Willard. *Headwaters of the Mississippi*. Chicago: Rand, McNally and Co., 1893.

Graves, Charles. *Leather Armchairs*. New York: Coward-McCann, 1964.

Havighurst, Walter. *Upper Mississippi: A Wilderness Saga*. New York: Farrar and Rinehart, 1937.

Heilbron, Bertha L. *The Thirty-second State*. St. Paul: Minnesota Historical Society, 1958.

Hill, Alfred J. "Constantine Beltrami." *Minnesota Historical*

Society Collections, II (1889), 183–96. (Reprint of 1867 article).

Holmquist, June Drenning. *History Along the Highways: An Official Guide to Minnesota—State Markers and Monuments.* St. Paul: Minnesota Historical Society, 1967.

James, Edwin. *Account of an Expedition from Pittsburgh to the Rocky Mountains, Performed in the Years 1819, and* 1820. 2 vols. Philadelphia: Carey and Lea, 1822–23. Reprint (Volume I). Cleveland: A. H. Clark and Co., 1905.

Jones, Evan. *Citadel in the Wilderness: The Story of Fort Snelling and the Northwest Frontier.* New York: Coward-McCann, 1966.

———. *The Minnesota: Forgotten River.* New York: Holt, Rinehart and Winston, 1962.

Keating, William H. *Narrative of an Expedition to the Source of St. Peter's River, Lake Winnepeek, Lake of the Woods, &c.* 2 vols. 1824. Reprint (2 vols. in 1). Minneapolis: Ross and Haines, 1959.

Kelsey, Vera. *Red River Runs North!* New York: Harper and Brothers, 1951.

Kennedy, Roger G. *Men on the Moving Frontier.* Palo Alto, Calif.: American West Publishing Co., 1969.

Lami, A. *Costantino Beltrami e la Scoperta delle Sorgenti del Mississippi.* Torino: G. C. Paravia, 1931.

Lee, Vernon [Viola Paget]. *The Countess of Albany.* Boston: Roberts Brothers, 1885.

Le Savoureux, H. *Chateaubriand.* Paris: Rieder, 1930.

Long, Stephen H. *Voyage in a Six-oared Skiff to the Falls of Saint Anthony in 1817.* Philadelphia: Henry B. Ashmead, 1860. 2nd ed. St. Paul: Minnesota Historical Society, 1889.

Martini, Ferdinando. "Donne, Salotti e Costumi." *La Vita Italiana Durante la Rivoluzione e l'Impero.* Milan: Fratelli Treves, 1931.

Martino, Pierre. "A Propos du Voyage en Amérique de Chateaubriand." *Revue d'Histoire Littéraire.* 1909, pp. 429–78.

Masi, Eugenia. *Giacomo Costantino Beltrami e le sue Esplorazioni in America.* Florence: G. Barbera,1902.

Merrick, George B. *Old Times on the Upper Mississippi:*

The Recollections of a Steamboat Pilot from 1854–1863. Cleveland: Arthur H. Clark Company, 1909.

Moroni, Pietro. *De' Viaggi e degli Scritti di G. C. Beltrami da Bergamo.* Bergamo: Pagnoncelli, 1865.

Morrison, William. "Who Discovered Itasca Lake?" *Minnesota Historical Society Collections,* I (1872), 417–19.

Neill, E. C. "Occurrences in and Around Fort Snelling, from 1819 to 1840." *Minnesota Historical Society Collections,* II (1865), 21–56.

_______. "A Sketch of Joseph Renville." *Minnesota Historical Society Collections,* I (1872), 196–206.

Nicollet, Joseph N. "Report Intended to Illustrate a Map of the Hydrographic Basin of the Upper Mississippi River," *Senate Documents,* 26th Cong., 2nd Sess., No. 237, pp. 53–74. Also in *House Documents,* 28th Cong., 2nd Sess., No. 52.

Paxton, John Adems. *The New Orleans Directory and Register.* New Orleans: 1822, 1823, 1824.

Penderson, Kern. *The Story of Fort Snelling.* St. Paul: Minnesota Historical Society, 1966.

Pennesi, Giuseppe. "Costantino Beltrami alla Ricerca delle Sorgenti del Mississippi." *Societa Geografica Italiana,* XX (1886), 444–80.

Petersen, Willian J. "The 'Virginia,' the 'Clermont' of the Upper Mississippi." *Minnesota Historical Society, Quarterly Magazine,* IX (1928), 347–62.

Phillips, Paul Chrisler. *The Fur Trader.* Norman: University of Oklahoma Press, 1961.

Pike, Zebulon Montgomery. *The Journals of Zebulon Montgomery Pike, with Letters and Related Documents.* Ed. Donald Jackson. 2 vols. Norman: University of Oklahoma Press, 1966.

Rosa, Gabriele. *Della Vita e degli Scritti di Costantino Beltrami da Bergamo Scopritore delle Fonti del Mississippi.* Bergamo: Pagnoncelli, 1861.

Saum, Lewis O. *The Fur Trader and the Indian.* Seattle: University of Washington Press, 1965.

Schiavo, Giovanni. "With Beltrami at the Headwaters of the

Mississippi River." *Atlantica,* January, 1931, pp. 9–12.

Schoolcraft, Henry R. *Narrative Journal of Travels Through the Northwestern Regions of the United States Extending from Detroit Through the Great Chain of American Lakes to the Sources of the Mississippi River in the Year 1820.* Ed. Mentor L. Williams. East Lansing: Michigan State University Press, 1953.

———. *Schoolcraft's Expedition to Lake Itasca: The Discovery of the Source of the Mississippi.* Ed. Philip P. Mason. East Lansing: Michigan State University Press, 1958.

Severin, Timothy. *Explorers of the Mississippi.* New York: Alfred A. Knopf, 1968.

———. "The Preposterous Pathfinder." *American Heritage,* 1967, pp. 56–63.

Sibley, Henry H. "Memoir of Jean N. Nicollet." *Minnesota Historical Society Collections,* I (1872), 183–95.

Taliaferro, Lawrence. "Auto-Biography of Major Lawrence Taliaferro—Written in 1864." *Minnesota Historical Society Collections,* VI (1894), 189–255.

Terrell, John Upton. *Furs by Astor.* New York: William Morrow and Company, 1963.

Thompson, David. *Thompson's Narrative, 1784–1812.* Ed. Richard Glover. Toronto: Champlain Society, 1962.

United States, Department of State. *Passengers Who Arrived in the United States: September 1821–December 1823.* Baltimore: Magna Carta Book Co., 1969.

Upham, Warren. *Minnesota in Three Centuries, 1655–1908.* 4 vols. St. Paul: Publishing Society of Minnesota, 1908.

Van Cleve, Charlotte O. "A Reminiscence of Ft. Snelling." *Minnesota Historical Society Collections,* VIII (1870), 76–81.

Vandersluis, Charles S. *A Brief History of Beltrami County.* Bemidji, Minn.: Beltrami County Historical Society, 1963.

Vertova, Camozzi, *Notizie e Lettere Pubblicate per Cura del Municipio di Bergamo e Dedicate alla Societa' Storica di Minnesota.* Bergamo: Pagnoncelli, 1865.

Wood, Richard G. *Stephen Harriman Long, 1784–1864:*

Army Engineer, Explorer, Inventor. Glendale, Calif.: Arthur H. Clark Company, 1966.

Woodall, Allen E. "William Joseph Snelling and the Early Northwest." *Minnesota Historical Society Quarterly Magazine,* (1929), 367–85.

Zavatti, Silvio. "La Persecuzione di Costantino Beltrami." *Giornale di Bergamo,* November 10, 1968, p. 15.

Ziebarth, Marilyn and Ominsky, Alan. *Fort Snelling: Anchor Post of the Northwest.* St. Paul: Minnesota Historical Society, 1970.

INDEX

Index

Typical presentation, if idealized, of an Indian, by an unknown painter in the 1820s.